THE
MINISTRY
OF THE
Husband

FOREWORD BY **REV. SIMON AMPOFO**

THE
MINISTRY
OF THE
Husband

Understanding Your Calling

DOUGLAS ASANTE

EQUIP
PUBLISHING
HOUSE

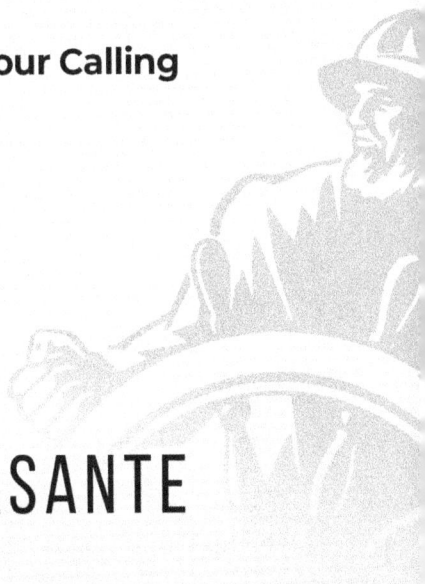

THE MINISTRY OF THE HUSBAND:
UNDERSTANDING YOUR CALLING

Copyright © 2024 by **Douglas Asante**

ISBN
978-1-916692-03-9

COVER/LAYOUT DESIGN
Bright Amoako-Attah

EDITING
Mrs. Rita Agyei-Poku

Email the author via **info@dasante.org.uk**
Visit website for more info **www.dasante.org.uk**

Unless otherwise indicated, quotations are taken from the New King James Version (NKJV) © 1982

Published in the United Kingdom by
Equip Publishing House

EQUIP
PUBLISHING
HOUSE

Asante

Dedication

To my beloved wife Diana Ama Asante,

In the intricate chapters of life, you are the inspiration that breathes purpose into my journey. Your unwavering faith and boundless love have guided me through the pages of our marriage, just as the guiding hand of the Almighty leads His flock.

This book, *"The Ministry of the Husband,"* is a testament to the sacred covenant we share and the profound wisdom that love, faith, and partnership bring to the institution of marriage. Your grace, patience, and devotion have illuminated the path for me to fulfill my role as a husband, and I dedicate these words to you, my cherished companion on this sacred odyssey.

May our love continue to be a shining beacon of God's grace, illuminating the hearts and minds of those who seek to understand the divine ministry of marriage.

With all my love and every blessing,

Douglas.

Contents

Endorsements

In an era where the foundations of family life seem to be constantly challenged, Reverend Douglas Asante's book, "*The Ministry of the Husband*," offers a refreshing and insightful perspective on the role of a husband within the context of Christian marriage. As a friend and fellow believer, I am honoured to endorse this remarkable work.

Reverend Asante's book goes beyond the traditional understanding of a husband's responsibilities and delves into the deep spiritual significance of his role. With wisdom, compassion, and a profound understanding of biblical principles, he navigates the complexities of modern relationships in light of the firmly rooted, timeless truths found in God's Word.

One of the book's greatest strengths is its emphasis on the concept of ministry within marriage. Reverend Asante beautifully highlights the idea that a husband's role extends far beyond mere provision and leadership. He illuminates the profound impact a husband can have on his wife's spiritual journey, nurturing her growth, and supporting her in becoming the woman God intended her to be.

Throughout the pages, readers will find practical guidance and thought-provoking reflections, equipping husbands with the tools they need to cultivate a Christ-centered home. The author addresses common challenges faced by husbands today, such as communication breakdowns, conflicts, and the balancing act of work and family life. With grace and humility, he offers valuable insights and actionable advice to help husbands navigate these challenges with wisdom and love.

What sets this book apart is the author's ability to balance deep theological insights with a relatable writing style. Whether you are a newlywed, a seasoned husband, or preparing for marriage, the author's words will resonate with your heart and guide you in creating a harmonious, loving, and God-honouring marriage.

The Ministry of the Husband is a powerful resource that will inspire husbands to embrace their calling with renewed dedication and purpose.

I wholeheartedly recommend this book to anyone seeking to strengthen their role as a Christian husband and cultivate a marriage that reflects the love and grace of Christ.

May this book find its way into the hands of many husbands, empowering them to embark on a lifelong journey of ministry within their homes and leaving a lasting impact on their wives, children, and future generations.

DR. ALEX PHIRI

Lead Minister at River of Life Community Church, Sheffield, and Principal of Emmaus School of Theology, Sheffield

The Ministry of the Husband by Douglas Asante shows Christian men how to be more than just seed donors and breadwinners. It reveals God's plan for their roles in the family. Did you know that a Christian husband is a gardener? Find out more in this book.

This book is a must-read for Christian husbands and fathers who want to apply the scriptural lessons in their lives. It is also for wives who want strong, happy and godly marriages.

ELD. CHARLES ANTO

Scientist, Church Leader, Experienced Marriage and Family Counsellor and Professional Speaker

God made marriage for the husband and wife to help each other. The book *The Ministry of the Husband* by Reverend Asante teaches the man how to be a head just like Christ, who sacrificed himself for his bride. This book is for every husband or future husband who wants a godly marriage.

DR. (MRS.) GRACE ASANTE-DUAH
Professional Woman, Wife, Mother, Writer and Speaker

The Ministry of the Husband by Douglas Asante is a manual for Christian husbands at any stage in their marriages. It teaches them how to be humble leaders in their homes based on the scriptures. It can be used for self-study, Bible study groups, seminars and sermons. It can be read alone or with *The Ministry of the Wife*. It is a great book for any Christian's library!

DR. (MRS.) LAEG
Medical Doctor, Church Deaconess, Wife and Mother

In these times that society is confused about the role of the man in the home, Douglas Asante brings illuminating biblical insights on this important subject through *The Ministry of the Husband*. This book is a must-read!

REV. OLIVIA OWUSU-SEKYERE
Senior Associate Pastor, Word of Faith Mission (UK)

The Ministry of the Husband by Douglas Asante shows how a man can be a gentle and humble leader in his family according to God's will. It is a simple and practical guide for men who want to be good husbands and fathers.

MRS. YVONNE ADADE
Philanthropist, Wife and Mother

The Ministry of the Husband is a God-inspired book that teaches the role of the man in a Christian marriage. It has practical examples and scriptural wisdom. It is a must-read for all men who want to honour God and bless their families.

DR. MARIAN ASAMOAH-ANIM
President, Jesus is Lord Crusades

Acknowledgements

In the journey of writing *"The Ministry of the Husband,"* I have been blessed with the support and guidance of many individuals who have contributed to this work in countless ways. Their unwavering faith and encouragement have been the cornerstone of this project, and I am deeply grateful.

First and foremost, I would like to express my heartfelt thanks to our Heavenly Father, whose wisdom and grace have illuminated this path. Without His divine inspiration, this book would not have been possible.

I am indebted to my loving wife, Diana, for her unwavering support, patience, and understanding throughout this writing process. Your constant encouragement and prayers have been my source of strength.

To my precious daughters, Dasha, Daphne, and Danelle, I extend my thanks for your encouragement and for allowing me to be a guiding light in your lives.

To Rev. Simon Ampofo, Dr. Alex Phiri, Elder Charles Anto, Dr. Mrs. Laeg, Dr. Grace Asante-Duah, Dr. Marian Asamoah-Anim, Rev. Olivia Owusu-Sekyere and Mrs. Yvonne Adade who have cheered me on and believed in the importance of this message, I extend my sincere appreciation. Your enthusiasm, input and encouragement have been a driving force.

My deepest gratitude goes to Rev. Mike Tembo, Pastor Nana Asante, and the devoted members of Christian Family Ministries for their unwavering support and dedication. Your commitment to this ministry and your fervor for God's word have enriched this book in immeasurable ways.

A special acknowledgment is reserved for the editorial and design team at Equip Publishing House, whose expertise and guidance have polished the essence of this book. Your discerning eyes and thoughtful suggestions have been priceless.

Finally, to all those who embark on this journey with open hearts, may God's blessings and revelations accompany you as you delve into the pages of *"The Ministry of the Husband."*

May this book serve as a wellspring of inspiration, counsel, and encouragement for all who seek to fulfill their divine calling as husbands, guided by the teachings of our Lord and Savior, Jesus Christ.

In His service,

Douglas Asante.

Foreword

I have known Douglas Asante for some years now, just around the time he tied the knot with his dear wife Diana. Together with his wife, they have kept close contact as spiritual children over the years. Douglas' maturity in the faith over the years has translated into all other aspects of his life, and this is remarkable.

His love and passion for God, family and ministry is sincere. I've seen him shepherd his family in the ways of God and I know this book *The Ministry of a Husband*, is borne out of Scripture and out of a life that he himself exemplifies.

I find the title of this book *The Ministry of a Husband* apt, because being a husband, and especially a godly husband, goes beyond a title or position, it's a real ministry. Many are called husbands but few are truly husbands. You just have to take a look at society today, and see that many men are not being the husbands their wives need. It takes more than six packs, fine suits or sleek cars to be a husband, and as Douglas shows us, to know how to be a husband, one has to go to the source and originator of marriage—God.

In this book, Douglas shows us that the first and most important duty of the man is to lead. Husband means head of the house. If the head fails to lead, imagine the confusion this will create. Unfortunately, many men have failed to lead, resulting in many dysfunctional homes. Oh, that men would rise up, and take up the mantle of leadership in their homes!

Another thing you will find intriguing in this book is some misconceptions about marriage that Douglas mentions. In my many years in pastoral ministry, I've been saddened by the misconceptions that people have and carry into their marriages, sometimes unknowingly. If only they knew, but alas! They go along with these wrong thoughts and end up hurting their marriages. This book will help you identify some of these misconceptions and help you understand what God's intention for marriage is, so you can travel the right path armed with the right information.

As the man, you should never forget that you wear many hats – provider, teacher, priest and a cultivator, which Douglas refers to in his book as a gardener. You are a cultivator because your wife is your God-given garden and you have been assigned to cultivate her. You want your wife to glow? Water her, prune her, feed her and see her flourish and thrive.

Having been married for over 20 years, I can confidently say that being a husband is a huge calling, a divine ministry that is not for the fickle and fainthearted. The good news is that resources abound to help you succeed in your calling, and one of such resources is this book, *The Ministry of the Husband*. Read it, learn from it, apply it and see your life become better.

I see you fulfilling your ministry as a husband. I see your wife and children praising you and celebrating you for the great husband and father that you will be!

Enjoy the book.

REV. SIMON AMPOFO
General Overseer, Gracefields Chapel

Introduction

Interestingly, all creatures, except humans, are a product of God's spoken word. He spoke, and creation came into existence. All things were made by God's invisible words (Colossians 1:16). When He was done, God saw that everything was excellent and perfect.

Is it not amazing to know that God created the world within six days? He made all things, and nothing has gone out of place ever since. Day and night have never changed. The fish of the sea, the animals of the land, and the birds of the air still exist where God originally intended (Genesis 1:1-20). What an awesome God He is!

God needed a representative on earth. He wanted someone who could hear His voice from heaven and re-echo it on earth and in whose hands He could entrust His beautiful works for generations to come. So, God made man to oversee His work on earth.

> 'Then God said, 'Let Us make man in
> Our image, according to Our likeness;
> let them have dominion over the fish of the sea,
> over the birds of the air, and over the cattle,

over all the earth and over every
creeping thing that creeps on the earth.'

GENESIS 1:26

God created all things by His Word. Yet, when creating man, He took a different approach (Genesis 1:27, Genesis 2:7). God is the architect of man's design; He made man Himself and He gave man His Spirit. Man was made to be like God on earth.

The scriptures say that as God is in heaven, so is man on earth (1 John 4:17, Isaiah 55:8, 9). The redeemed man has God's virtues, honour, and characteristics. He has the Spirit of God inside him. God invested the spirit of wisdom, right counsel, understanding, strength, knowledge, and the fear of the Lord (Isaiah 11:1-3) in man. Hence, man is an embodiment of the Spirit of God on earth. Man emulates the personality of God so much that the angels question his existence:

> *'What is man that You are mindful of*
> *him and the son of man that You visit him?*
> *For You have made him a little lower than*
> *the angels (meaning Elohim in the Hebrew*
> *rendition), and You have crowned him with*
> *glory and honour. You have made him have*

dominion over the works of Your hands;
You have put all things under his feet.'

PSALMS 8:4-6

God (Elohim) made man a little lower than Himself. The man was made with a distinct feature - his body (flesh). Man's body is what makes him a legal entity on earth. Therefore, man is both a physical and spiritual being.

First, let's have the understanding that man refers to the spirit in the male, and the female. Since a spirit has no gender, it is the container (body) the spirit assumes or resides in that defines them as male or female. *When God created man, we saw the manifestation of the male, then the female. With no intent of making less of the 'female man', the word 'man' used throughout this book is in reference to the male man in order not to confuse the reader.*

The truth is that being a 'man' exceeds having a masculine figure and the ability to father a child. A man is God's representative on earth and is given dominion over all that God created. "The man" — the male — is the manager of God's resources on earth. Therefore, being a man implies the responsibility of living a life in service to God.

Though the male was made to lead and have dominion over all that God had created, God knew he could not do it alone. Therefore, God gave him a woman to become one with him so they could work together as a team to fulfil God's will on earth. A man must always see his wife as his teammate and not as a property or someone lower to him in creation. God showed us the power of teamwork when He said, *'Let us make man in our own image...'*

A husband needs a teammate to fulfil God's mandate of fruitfulness, dominion and increase on the earth. Therefore, a man's wife is his greatest strength for leadership and headship.

Man was made in Eden (Genesis 2:8), which I think was never a physical location but God's presence. It is a place where man must dwell continuously if he ever wants to become who God intends for him to be. Any husband who wants to lead outside Eden may end up putting nations and generations into error. The more he looks to God and stays in His presence, the more man becomes like God, and the better he can lead his home in the right direction.

How well can one manage God's creatures and resources without a relationship with the Creator? How well can one know him or herself without the Creator? What do we know about our purpose, calling and assignment on earth?

We must understand that a man is not fit to step into the shoes of a husband until God grooms him into manhood.

Being a husband is part of God's plan for every man. As husbands, we must see our role in the home as a ministry. We are called into this ministry of a husbandman. Within this husbandry is where we establish one of the greatest assignments on earth.

A husband is the father of many nations. God is more concerned about the nations that will arise from you. He could trust the man Jacob with the 12 tribes of Israel. How much can God entrust into your hands?

This book is a call for every husband to rise to their responsibility. As you read the pages of this book, you will understand your identity in God and the assignment He placed into your hands.

Please take your time to prayerfully read this book as it contains the Word of God, which will enable you to work in your divine office as a husband.

1

THE **CREATION**
OF THE **MAN**

CHAPTER ONE

The Creation of the Man

'So God created man in His own image;
In the image of God He created him,
male and female He created them.'

GENESIS 1:27

Who is man? What is he made of? What makes man unique in creation? Whose identity does he have? These questions border on the design and nature of man. It is good to know that, for certain, God created man for His purpose. So long as you are a man, your life is unto God.

Man was made in the image of God to effectively carry out His assignment on earth. God gave man all he needed at creation to function in his office and fulfil his purpose on earth. Therefore, what one becomes as a man is a result of the choices they make. God made man in His image, and he is expected to glorify Him. You are forged by the breath of God (Genesis 2:7). He made man and gave him His Spirit so that as He is in heaven, the man could also live in the same capacity on earth. Man is God's representative to the world, and we must not fail in our assignment.

MAN'S COMPOSITION

'And the Lord God formed man out of the dust of the ground, and breathed into his nostrils the breath of life, and man became a living soul.'

GENESIS 2:7

God took the dust of the earth and formed man's flesh or physical matter. However, his flesh is not the only component that makes up his entire being. The man has other components. Without these components, he is incomplete.

From the onset, the source of the creation story—the Bible— makes us understand that God breathed into man the breath of life. The Bible continues by telling us that man became a living soul after receiving the breath of God. This indicates or suggests that the two components:

4

body and soul, came together to make man come alive. However, that is not the entire composition of man. There is a third component, his spirit.

> *'And the very God of peace sanctify you*
> *wholly; and I pray God your whole spirit,*
> *soul and body be preserved blameless unto*
> *the coming of our Lord Jesus Christ.'*
>
> 1 THESSALONIANS 5:23

The above Bible text by Apostle Paul clearly distinguishes man's spirit from his soul. Paul makes this distinction clearer in this letter to the Thessalonian church. He distinguishes the spirit (pneuma) from the soul (psyche) and the body (soma).

> *'For the Word of God is quick, and powerful,*
> *sharper than any two-edged sword, piercing*
> *even to the dividing asunder of soul and spirit,*
> *and the joints and marrow and is a discerner*
> *of the thoughts and intents of the heart.'*
>
> HEBREWS 4:12

The body is the physical component of the man and can be seen and touched. The soul and spirit are man's immaterial components, consisting of a will, emotions, conscience, mind, and heart. The spirit, soul and body combine to form man's humanity.

The Body (Soma)

The body is man's material or physical aspect, which connects man to his physical environment. One interacts with the earth's realm through their sight, senses of smell, touch, taste and through sound.

The body is man's outer component. It makes him susceptible to sin due to its sensations (desires, cravings, and lust). To live according to God's Word, we must control our flesh's sensations. Without controlling these bodily urges, one is bound to fall into sin. Sin keeps us from manifesting the true identity of God and inhibits our ability to fulfil our role as husbands.

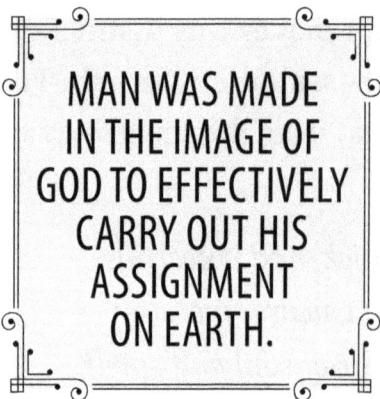

> MAN WAS MADE IN THE IMAGE OF GOD TO EFFECTIVELY CARRY OUT HIS ASSIGNMENT ON EARTH.

The Bible talks about the need to guard the body against sin in 1 Corinthians 6:20:

'For ye are bought with a price: therefore glorify God in your body and in your spirit, which are God's.'

The body is the home of the spirit and the soul. As such, it has to be kept in pure condition for God's use. Again, the Bible bolsters the importance of keeping the body free from sin.

It says, *'Do you not know that you are the temple of God and that the Spirit of God dwells in you? If anyone defiles the temple of God, God will destroy him. For the temple of God is holy, which temple you are.'*

1 CORINTHIANS 3:16-17

To be successful in this ministry as a man and as a husband, one must dedicate the body to God. God is pure. Practising purity makes one a useful vessel in His vineyard. We must stay pure to access more profound mysteries from God for life, family, and ministry.

Promiscuity and all forms of licentiousness break homes and damage many things within households, including children's destinies. We must not trade our future or that of our children for pleasure that will be short-lived.

The Soul (psyche)

The soul is the first of the immaterial components of man. The soul of man is that component that makes him a living entity on earth. In Genesis 2:7, the Bible tells us that when the breath of life was passed into man, he became a **living soul**. The man's soul makes him perceive danger, safety, joy, and other such emotions within himself and others.

The soul gives man his personality. Your behaviour is a function of what has happened in your soul. Your soul learns what the body cannot understand, and through mindfulness and meditation, it grows to become more sensitive. The soul consists of self-awareness, reason, volition, conscience and emotion. The soul can be grouped into three main parts: the mind, will and emotion.

The mind has two parts: the conscious and the subconscious parts. Consciousness is being capable of thought and reason, while the subconsciousness consists of our emotions and beliefs. Additionally, feelings and memories are present in our subconsciousness. On the other hand, the will is your ability to make choices.

As said earlier, the soul cannot be seen or touched, but it is a crucial component of man. One can develop their soul to know more profound things over time. Exposure to different environments affects the workings of the soul. The soul may be ignorant, and after exposure to knowledge, it becomes wise. Wisdom helps the soul make good choices (will).

> *'But the natural man does not receive the things of the Spirit of God, for they are foolishness to him; nor can he know them, because they are spiritually discerned.'*
>
> 1 CORINTHIANS 2:14

The soul is the meeting point; here the spirit and the body join. The soul lies in between these two worlds and belongs to these two worlds. On one hand, it communicates with the spiritual realm through the spirit, and on the other hand, it communicates with the physical world through the body. However, when one schools their soul on the Word of God, it begins to learn the language of the Spirit.

The Spirit (Pneuma)

'The Spirit itself bears witness with our spirits, that we are children of God.'

ROMANS 8:16

Since the fall of Adam, the human spirit has become alienated from God. The sin in Eden brought a barrier in fellowship between God and man. So, the spirit died due to sin. However, through the death and resurrection of Jesus, we can all have access to God with our spirit, which, through the Holy Spirit, is made alive in Christ Jesus through our belief in His death and confession of His resurrection.

'And if Christ is in you, the body is dead because of sin; but the spirit is life because of righteousness.'

ROMAN 8:10

The spirit deals with the flesh's sin and makes you live life to please God alone. A man of the Spirit knows God's mind and hears, understands and obeys the counsel of

God. A man who consistently walks in the leadings of the Holy Spirit will lead his family right.

FOUNDATIONS OF MAN'S IDENTITY

A man who doesn't know his identity suffers from an 'identity crisis.' This person lacks information about what makes him different, where he comes from, what motivates him, and the foundations upon which his sense of 'self' should be built.

A man's identity informs him about who he is, where he comes from and what he does. The characteristics, feelings, and beliefs of the man make him unique from any other creature. And yet, every man has a unique personality that makes him different from others.

Aside from the identity crisis which a man who doesn't know who he is may suffer, a man may also have false identities. False identities stem from not knowing who one is, or, worse still, knowing the truth but ignoring it, and choosing to mirror another person's characteristics and attributes. These two issues are the identity problems that an unbeliever or a non-Christian man struggles with most of their life on earth. When one does not know himself through God, how, then, do they define their identity? What are the ways one can sum up the things that define us as men?

The world, using different criteria, has many ways of defining a man's identity. These include, but are not limited to, the roles on his CV or resume, his lineage, achievements or failures and job history. One may also define the man's identity based on political ideologies: a democrat, a communist, or a republican. Wealth or lack of it has also been used to classify or categorise men into the rich or the poor. Also, sickness or affliction and sin are often used to brand people: a cancer patient, a disabled man, an angry person, or an addict.

A believer who does not know who he is might suffer from an identity crisis or a false identity. It is common to see believers today define themselves by church denominations or their gifts and talents.

All these ways have been the world's view of a person's identity. But these categorisations have nothing to do with God, the Creator of all mankind. So, this leaves us with a big question: Who is the Christian man then? What is his identity? What can be used to figure out the Christian man's true essence?

Made in the Image of God

Every Christian man or husband has one identity. Yes, you read that right. Does it mean that all men have the same feelings, characteristics and composition? Not necessarily, but God does. And that is the only criteria to base a man's true identity.

In Genesis 1:26, the Bible gives us the first glimpse of man's identity. God said:

> *'Let's make man in our image, according to*
> *Our likeness; let them have dominion over the*
> *fish of the sea, over the birds of the air, over*
> *the cattle, over all the earth and over every*
> *creeping thing that creeps on the earth.'*

One's identity must be deeply embedded in the character of God. We are God's image made flesh. Thus, we bear the characteristics and attributes of our Maker. Society defines a man by his masculinity, muscles, pride, assertiveness, self-confidence, and, mostly, by his unemotional nature. However, these things do not represent a man's true identity. Such descriptions, categorisations or adjectives may not make a man build a successful home and understand his ministry as a husband.

> *'But when He saw the multitudes,*
> *He was moved with compassion for them,*
> *because they were weary and scattered,*
> *like sheep having no shepherd.'*
>
> MATTHEW 9:36

The attributes that help a man carry out his duty were seen in the man Jesus Christ when He came from heaven to earth to save humanity. The true identity of a man is demonstrated through his humility, dependence and submission to God during his time on earth. Jesus is compassionate, merciful, loving, forgiving, and decisive in His service to others. These are the characters and traits that define a man born of God.

For a man to fully express his God-given identity, he must submit to the will of God first. The Bible teaches us what submission to God's promises looks like. In James 4:7, the Bible says, '*Submit yourself to God, resist the devil, and he will flee from you*'. Jesus submitted to the will of God and showed man the perfect example of being submissive to God's will. This was possible for Jesus because He knew who He was.

> '*And being found in human form, He humbled Himself by becoming obedient to the point of death, even death on a cross.*'
>
> PHILIPPIANS 2:8

A husband who wants his wife to submit to him must first learn to submit to God. The Bible establishes that a man should submit to God and a woman to her husband (Ephesians 5:22-32).

Let's take another lesson from Jesus' life. There was a time when Jesus Christ became hungry after long days of fasting. Therefore, the devil thought he could take advantage of Christ the Messiah's vulnerability and strip Him of His identity. The Bible says:

> *"'Then the devil took Him up into the holy city, set Him on the pinnacle of the temple, and said to Him, 'If You are the Son of God, throw Yourself down. For it is written: 'He shall give His angels charge over You, and, 'in their hands, they shall bear You up, lest You dash Your foot against a stone. Jesus said to him, 'It is written again, 'You shall not tempt the Lord your God.'"*

MATTHEW 4:5-7

Amazing! Jesus's reply to the devil's gimmick was epic. A man created in God's image and likeness possesses the identity of God. Therefore, when the devil questions your fleshly lifestyle, it is his way of bringing you down. These traits include God's wisdom, kindness, guidance, care, protection, fatherly love, and teaching. Therefore, the man who possesses God's identity manifests these traits in his home.

A Child of God

*'For you are all sons of God through faith
in Christ Jesus. For as many of you as were
baptised into Christ have put on Christ.'*

GALATIANS 3:26-27

Man is something else too: he is a child of God.

A man's identity is further defined by his lineage. The lineage can be broken down into two types: the earthly lineage and the spiritual lineage. The earthly lineage is ephemeral. When a man's descent is wiped out, he struggles to identify where he is from and what he represents. Inasmuch as a man has an earthly family, he also has an eternal spiritual lineage, which is God's family.

A Christian man's lineage is always traced to God. When one becomes born again, he automatically enters God's lineage and is born into a new family. When a man is reborn into the family of God, he is given a new identity and a new Father. He becomes a child of God.

The Bible says:

*'I write unto you children because your
sins are forgiven you for His namesakes.'*

1 JOHN 2:14

The Bible continues in verse thirteen: *'I write unto you, little children because ye have known the Father.'*

Oh yes! We have a Father now. He is God, and there exists a Father-child relationship between God and us.

The new birth takes away the inherent nature of the previous life (2 Corinthians 5:17). We receive a new and unique nature that enables us to call on God and to tap into His blessings and forgiveness. At salvation, we become children of God.

Note this: our salvation is not by our effort or will. We are saved by the blood of Jesus through faith in His name.

The Bible says:

> *'But as many as received Him, to them He*
> *gave the right to become children of God,*
> *to those who believe in His name: who were*
> *not born of blood, nor of the will of the flesh,*
> *nor of the will of man, but of God.'*

JOHN 1:12-13

Through the new birth, we have access to God's gifts and His promises. Our Father-child relationship with God rests upon our faith in Jesus. This identity gives one the power to conquer sin and claim the victory in Christ Jesus.

A Father

'I have written unto you fathers because ye
have known Him that is from the beginning.'

1 JOHN 2:13, 14

Another aspect of our identity is that of a father. We are fathers not only because of our natural position and presence in the family, but also because of our knowledge of God. Biblical fatherhood is what qualifies us to influence others positively.

As Christian husbands, God expects us to point others to Him. But how can we reveal God to people when we do not know Him ourselves? This is why God desires that every man grows into spiritual maturity first before taking the position of a father. This maturity becomes part of our identity which is needed for our household's proper leadership.

In summation, first we are born again with God's spiritual identity, then we blossom as children under God's parental care. From there, we need to show others the fatherly nature of God. One of our responsibilities is to sow seeds of spiritual legacy into the children's heart, which makes us fathers.

'For whom the Lord loves He chastens,
and scourges every son whom He receives.'

HEBREWS 12:6

Fatherhood is double-sided. It is both an expression of love and a rod of correction. We demonstrate our love by the way we correct the wrongs in our household and community. As a father, one must learn to correct in love. We must not allow our emotions to control and override our sense of judgement.

A good father learns and exercises mastery over his emotions. One's ability to correct in love will make the child see the rod of correction as a sign of discipline, instead of hatred. Just like God corrects us when we err, we also need to bring the corrective rod to our homes. We build people when we correct them in love.

A child grows into maturity by both nurturing and correction. As fathers, every man should be responsible for this. We must know when to pat and when to correct. And we must always do it out of love.

The reason God will not commit deep things into the hands of some men is that they have not allowed Him to walk them into the full expression of manhood. If God can trust one's fatherhood, then He can entrust to that man's care, gifted and anointed children who will impact the world for the advancement of God's kingdom.

By leading others to God, a man demonstrates to the world and indeed, himself, that he lives out the faith he professes. God wants us to be fathers who can lead others by our godly lifestyle. Therefore, we need God to work on us to reflect what He wants to make out of us or see in us —a faithful father.

Often, I tell young ladies never to marry someone who has not been worked on by God. Someone who is not born again, has not yielded to the leadership of the Holy Spirit and is not Spirit-controlled.

God had to work on Adam before He gave him Eve (Genesis 2:18-23). God gave Adam responsibilities and planted him in the Garden of Eden. Adam's obedience to his assignment and his ability to remain where he was first planted despite his aloneness, were all part of the workings God had to take Adam through.

The Christian man's identity does not stem from his physical environment or opinions of others. He is beyond the afflictions he encounters. Our identity is found in God alone. We are the image of God and His children. Subsequently, God has made us fathers to others. The Christian man first needs to be born again to regain his God-given identity. Only then, can he become a child of God and grow into maturity to become a father to others.

HIS DUTIES

> *'Then God said, 'Let Us make man in Our image, according to Our likeness; let them have dominion over the fish of the sea, over the birds of the air, and over the cattle, over all the earth and over every creeping thing that creeps on the earth.'*

GENESIS 1:26

Man's creation was not an afterthought. God created man last, so the earth was prepared ahead of him.

Even before the creation of man, his duties had been made clear. Man would be a custodian of every other living thing created by God. Therefore, man is primarily a leader.

Lead

The first and most important duty of the man is to lead. The man is the head of the family. One abandons God's mandate for his life as a man when he abdicates that leadership position to someone else in the family. We are the head in our homes. However, being the 'head' does not signify male dominance, as many people often misuse the term these days.

Headship signifies leadership. A good leader does not dominate those he leads. Jesus Christ gave the perfect description of leadership when he said:

'And whoever desires to be first among you, let him be your slave — just as the Son of Man did not come to be served, but to serve, and to give His life a ransom for many.'

MATTHEW 20:27-28

Leadership is about service. We need to commit ourselves to serving our homes. Go the extra mile for the family. With every task, the man is to lead the way for the family and be an example; a leader is a doer.

A true leader asks questions and gets others' opinions. Leadership values cooperation and understanding rather than bossiness. A man called to serve as a leader shares responsibilities with his wife and children at home. He sees his family as a team.

The man's leadership is ordained by God (1 Corinthian 11:3). The man lives with his wife according to God's principles. He coordinates the affairs in the home and makes sure things are done well and in order. The husband provides a sense of direction for other members of the family. He leads, and the others follow.

The man is just like the shepherd who leads and guides the flock, giving guidance and instruction. To this end, the Bible instructs the woman to recognise the leadership of the man. Hence, there should be no struggle for that leadership position in the home. The leadership position in the home is solely the man's responsibility, irrespective of his personality.

The man is the source of spiritual, financial, emotional and psychological leadership. He provides godly headship for the family so that they follow God's instructions. The leader in the home points his family to God. The Bible testifies of Abraham:

> 'For I have known him, so that he may
> command his children and his household after
> him, that they keep the way of the Lord, to do
> righteousness and justice, that the Lord may
> bring to Abraham what He has spoken to him.'
>
> GENESIS 18:19

Amazing! God recognised Abraham as a good leader because he taught his household well. The best gift any man can give to his home is showing them how to have a relationship with God. But how will that happen if the man himself does not have a relationship with God? Do we share God's Word in our homes? When last did we have a quiet time? When was the last time we prayed for our wives? Think about these things.

Know Your Home

What do you know about your wife? Would you realise it when she is happy or sad? What do you think gives her joy in the home? You need to know your wife well to lead your family well.

The knowledge a man has about his wife helps him manage the home's affairs. Without this knowledge, the man will struggle to lead successfully. Just as a shepherd knows his sheep, so is the husband expected to know his wife. We ought to know the likes and dislikes, strengths and weaknesses, preferences and aversions, and, most importantly, how deeply rooted our wives are in God. Our familiarity with our wife's personality will help us manage situations in the home properly. Also, our knowledge about our wife strengthens the core of friendship that exists between us.

'I am the good shepherd, I know my sheep, and I am known of mine. My sheep hear my voice, and I know them, and they follow me.'

JOHN 10: 27-28

The sheep follows the shepherd primarily because the shepherd establishes a bond with them. He knows his flock, and they follow his voice. One should know each member of their family, individually. Study their different personalities and appreciate who they are individually.

This knowledge makes it easier to relate with each member of the family. Winning their hearts also becomes easier. Altogether, this makes the headship role of the man easy.

Love Your Wife

One of the greatest commandments and illustrations of man's love is to love his neighbour as he loves himself.

> 'And the second, like it, is this: 'You shall love your neighbour as yourself. There is no other commandment greater than these.'
>
> MARK 12:31

However, that is not yet the best illustration of love. There is a more excellent form of love Jesus showed when He came to die for us (John 13:34). He commanded us to love unconditionally just as He loved us.

In the letter to the Ephesians, Paul relates the love of Jesus to the love a husband needs to show his wife.

> 'Husbands love your wives, even as Christ also loved the church, and gave Himself for it.'
>
> EPHESIANS 5:25

The love that Jesus has for the church is unconditional. Similarly, it becomes the husband's responsibility to love his wife unconditionally. The love of a husband for his wife should not be based on how well she behaves towards you or on how well she performs her duties. Instead, the man must see her as a precious gift from God, and he must love God's gift to him. Husbands must affirm their love both with actions and words as often as they can. The best way to show love is not by words alone but by actions.

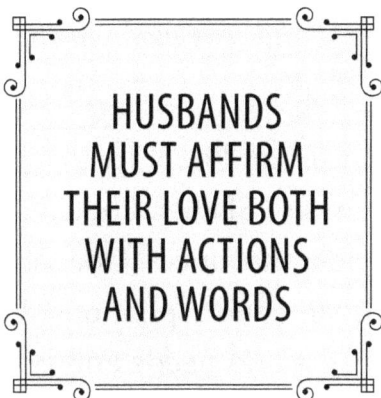

> **HUSBANDS MUST AFFIRM THEIR LOVE BOTH WITH ACTIONS AND WORDS**

*'My little children let us not love in word,
neither in tongue; but in deed and truth.'*

1 JOHN 3:18

The author of the book *Five Love Languages*, Gary Chapman, mentioned **words of affirmation** and **gifts** as part of the love languages we must speak to our spouse. Learn her love language and communicate it to her often.

Serve

The leadership of the home is more than giving instructions and guidance. It involves service. Only those who have learnt to serve others can genuinely lead people. As head of the church, Christ showed the perfect example of leadership when He washed the disciples' feet. He served. His coming down to earth to die for us was an act of service.

'But made Himself of no reputation,
and took upon Him the form of a servant,
and was made in the likeness of men.'

PHILIPPIANS 2:7

A husband's ability to understand his wife's needs helps him serve better. Endeavour to know her feelings, desires, and annoyances. Does she need anything? What are her dreams and aspirations? We should be aware of our wife's wants and needs and be available whenever she needs help. By doing this, we demonstrate that we are caring or supportive husbands and leaders.

Provide

'But if any provide not for his own, and
especially for those of his own house, he hath
denied the faith, and is worse than an infidel.'

I TIMOTHY 5:8

The Bible text above cannot be overemphasised. As men, we must provide for the needs of our wife. Making provision for the family is one of the many ways of serving and it is a fundamental part of a man's leadership role.

As the husband of the home, it is expected that we meet not only our wife's material and financial needs, but also to go beyond her earthly needs; we are expected to provide emotional support and spiritual support to the family.

Spiritual and emotional support are fundamental needs that a godly man provides for his wife, and his home.

The Commandments

Commandments are divine rules. Commandments are given to help guide an individual or a group's behaviour so that they become aligned with the will of God. As a husband, the Bible is your sole guide. Avoid consulting or resorting to the world system or to natural or carnal means for help. The world system is corrupt and has nothing good to offer. The world's idea of marriage is fundamentally flawed. Thankfully, the Bible has guidelines on how to succeed in the union.

There are no universities where a man can obtain a degree in marriage studies. Even professional marriage courses are not sufficient to help one build a successful home. A marital institution is a forever contract of two unique people coming to dwell under the same roof. Never think it takes just some certificate to sustain marriage. You will need something more.

This is why we need to know God's commandment concerning our marriage. Some of the commandments given to the husband regarding his ministry include the following:

Honour Your Wife

'Likewise, ye husbands, dwell with them according to knowledge, giving honour unto the wife, as unto the weaker vessel, and as being heirs together of the grace of life; that your prayers be not hindered.'

1 PETER 3:7

Honouring the wife means to treat her with respect, value and esteem. To value one's wife means placing importance on her. A man must treat his wife as an equal, not as a messenger. Despite being the head of the home, the Bible reiterates that all children of God are equal (Galatians 3:28).

When a man dishonours his wife, one of its consequence is that his prayers go unanswered. This illustrates how important it is for a man to respect and value the gift of a wife. God has entrusted into our hands the care of our wife, and we must take it seriously. To disregard her would be to ignore God's gift.

Work in Tandem with Your Wife

A marriage is a union between a man and a woman, a life-long team. For this team to achieve successful marriage goals, they must work together. One of the areas where teamwork is necessary is in establishing discipline in the home. As a man, you might be tempted to think that it is your duty and yours alone to establish rules in the home. But it is not. Both husband and wife have equal responsibility in creating rules that work for the home. Working together is one way to build a successful marriage. See yourselves as a team.

Some husbands relinquish their duty to raise godly children to their wives. This is not appropriate. As husbands, we should endeavour to be actively involved in bringing up our children in the ways of God. The more we work together, the better the children may become.

Put

When a man and his wife are joined in marriage, they form or become a new family, different from the one they individually share with their parents and siblings. As a husband, your allegiance is first and foremost to your wife, who has now become your immediate family.

> *'For this cause shall a man leave his father*
> *and mother, and shall be joined unto his wife,*
> *and they two shall be one flesh.'*
>
> EPHESIANS 5:31

The wife now becoming the man's immediate family is not to say that his extended family, including his parents, siblings, aunties, cousins, etc., has become irrelevant. Notwithstanding, he needs to understand that his first obligation is to his wife and his own children.

Love Your Wife

'Nevertheless, let every one of you in particular so love his wife even as himself; and the wife see that she reverence her husband.'

EPHESIANS 5: 33

God recognises the man as the head of the home and also explicitly commands him to love his wife without holding back. As the head, husbands are not expected to 'lord' over their wife. Instead, they are to love, protect, nourish and care for them. Love your wife as you love yourself.

However, loving your wife in a godly way is impossible unless you have a relationship with God. You cannot love yourself if you do not love God and spend time in His presence. God is love, and His love starts to manifest in you (Romans 5:5) when you spend time with Him.

Consequently, self-sacrifice is love: love that does not withhold anything from the other party (Ephesians 5:25). As a husband, this is what the Lord demands of you. Love your wife at all times without holding grudges. Always practise forgiveness. Therefore, you must never ridicule your wife or criticise her in public.

Love is also respecting your wife by recognising her opinion, realising when she is correct, and letting her tend the needs of the children. By doing these, you show respect for your wife. Be responsible enough to disagree with her and deal with it privately. Love your wife as Christ loved the church: purposefully, affectionately and sacrificially.

2

THE **PURPOSE** OF **MARRIAGE**

CHAPTER TWO

The Purpose of Marriage

"And He answered and said to them,
'Have you not read that He who made them
at the beginning 'made them male and
female, and said, 'For this reason, a man
shall leave his father and mother and be
joined to his wife, and the two shall become
one flesh'? So then, they are no longer two
but one flesh. Therefore what God has joined
together, let not man separate."

MATTHEW 19:4-6

The scripture above is an answer Jesus gave the Pharisees when they questioned if it was lawful to divorce or not. These Pharisees were not the only ones who sought some form of clarification regarding marriage. Many seek clarifications on what marriage is, what age is appropriate for one to get married, its purpose, who could marry, issues of polygamous marriage, the concepts of divorce and remarriage, among others. These and many other questions are the reasons for diverse and controversial opinions about the concept of marriage.

GOD'S WORD ABOUT MARRIAGE

The Bible says:

> 'All Scripture is given by inspiration of God, and is profitable for doctrine, for reproof, for correction, for instruction in righteousness, that the man of God may be complete, thoroughly equipped for every good work.'
>
> 2 TIMOTHY 3:16-17

The Bible is God's word and God's direction for living correctly. People were inspired by God's Spirit to document the Scriptures. So, the Bible serves as an instructional and divine tool for us.

Think about it: in order to understand the function of a piece of equipment or a product, you must first check the manufacturer's manual, which contains the creator's written instructions and descriptions the product's intended use. Likewise, you cannot know the meaning of marriage without first consulting the one who initiated it—God.

God instituted marriage right from the beginning of the human race. He saw the need for humanity to be fruitful and multiply and rule over all the world's nations. Therefore, right from Eden, God instituted the very first marital union. Since then, a God-ordained marriage has remained the standard that you and I must follow.

'Therefore, a man shall leave his father
and mother and be joined to his wife,
and they shall become one flesh. And they
were both naked, the man and his wife,
and were not ashamed.'

GENESIS 2:24-25

Amazing! The above Bible text speaks volumes about the purpose and principles of marriage. These will be discussed as we progress with this treatise. In the meantime, let us look at some misconceptions about marriage.

MISCONCEPTIONS ABOUT MARRIAGE

• Love is enough

Some people assume that love is the ultimate ingredient for marriage, but this is not true! As much as love is essential in marriage, trust, respect, and other such virtues are essential ingredients needed to make the relationship work, and to be more enjoyable. Love is the first step. However, you must develop communication skills, understanding, and allow the Spirit of God to find expression through you in all you do in your marriage.

At the start of the relationship, a man may fall in love with certain qualities in his wife. But what happens to that love when he begins to sees other aspects of his wife that are less desirable to him. This is why the Bible says:

> *'My little children, let us not love in word*
> *or in tongue, but in deed and in truth.'*
>
> 1 JOHN 3:18

Love, therefore, goes beyond the initial attraction and the beautiful words you say to your wife in marriage. Love is expressed by actions from a sincere heart. In marriage, you share love, bear each other's burden, and trust each other's decisions. Marriage and love require sacrifice that goes beyond mere infatuation.

• You will live happily ever after

Marriage has been reduced to fantasy and 'happily-ever-after' endings. The marriage portrayed in fictional movies is false because challenges are inevitable in life and marriage. Jesus said:

'These things I have spoken to you, that in
Me you may have peace. In the world you will
have tribulation, but be of good cheer,
I have overcome the world.'

JOHN 16:33

The marital home will experience attacks from the devil. There will be challenging and difficult times, but Jesus guarantees our safety.

The storms of life will blow. Sometimes, God will calm the storm. Other times, He will calm you down. Either way, know that God is with you in the midst of that trouble because He designed your marriage to stay strong through it all.

Consequently, as a husband, you must understand your wife. If not, petty arguments might break the home (1Peter 3:7). Never liken your marriage to romantic films. Although marriage has ingredients of romance, according to God's plan, that is not the ultimate for any marital bliss.

• Your spouse will make you complete

'…and you are complete in Him, who is
the head of all principality and power.'

COLOSSIANS 2:10

Dear husband and wife, always remember that you both are complete in Christ Jesus. Your identity is not in another person but Christ. You do not complete each other but complement each other in marriage. Do not make your wife feel she is nobody without you, which is incorrect. The joining together of the husband and his wife is a coming together of two whole persons under one umbrella, who is God Almighty.

• I can change him or her

This is mostly common with women who hope to change a man's attitude in marriage. However, some men also think they can change their spouse's attitude when they get married. But the truth of the matter is that what and who you are before the marriage ceremony is what and/ or who you remain in the marriage.

> *'Can the Ethiopian change his skin or the leopard its spots? Then may you also do good who are accustomed to do evil.'*

JEREMIAH 13:23

So, do not think you can change your spouse's personality in marriage. A woman who nags and complains before marriage will continue to do so in her marriage. Additionally, a man who easily gets angry will not change after the marriage ceremony. What changes people is the Spirit of God not their marital status.

• Marriage has no rules

You often hear people say that there are no rules in marriage. Hence, they do as they feel. Inasmuch as marriage does not take away your freedom and right, it does not also take away your sanity. The habit of clubbing, late-night movements, making careless speeches, and such attitudes that do not reveal God's intent for marriages should be avoided. Marriage has rules, and successful couples adhere to these rules strictly.

• You can replace your partner at will

The 21st Century is an era where some people shop for a spouse the same way they shop for shoes. Such people 'check out their size,' and if it does not fit, they simply try something else. When these kinds of people eventually find the one that suits them, they wear it for some time until it fades or goes out of style. Then, they throw it into the trash or keep it inside their closet and rush out to replace it. It is not uncommon to find such people quit their marriage at will because of one slight misunderstanding or the other.

God is not happy with divorce as it was never part of His plan. Marriage is eternal (Matthew

> **MARRIAGE HAS RULES, AND SUCCESSFUL COUPLES ADHERE TO THESE RULES STRICTLY**

19:6). You are not meant to be together for a while but forever – until separated by death. Therefore, jumping from one partner to another is contrary to the will of God.

• One person for every person

Now, I like to tell you that there is no one person for each individual because God did not prepare a woman specifically for you, whom you will one day meet and marry. Let us assume that this concept is true and then consider this analogy: if God has one person for each person, and they end up not marrying each other but someone else, then it holds that their error will affect the rest of humanity. One person's error will automatically break the chain. So, this misconception is never correct, and it is unbiblical.

Although God guides you in choosing who to marry, the decision to live with the person for the rest of your life is up to you. It is a choice.

Having understood the various misconceptions surrounding marriage, what then is the real purpose of marriage?

UNDERSTANDING GOD'S INTENTION FOR MARRIAGE

God does nothing without a reason. When you see God at work, know that He finished before starting—He already has a picture of the end result in mind before He starts working. The creation story is a vivid example of what I mean. The Bible says:

'In the beginning, God created the heavens and the earth.'

GENESIS 1:1

The scripture makes us understand that God created heaven and earth in the beginning. But God did not stop there. Since the picture God had in mind did not reflect in the creation, God went further to create many amazing things until He saw that they were good (Genesis 1:25).

After that, God went further to make man in His image. God made someone in His form, to look like God and have dominion on earth. In God's plan, He made man and created a woman for the man to live happily together.

Interestingly, marriage began in Eden when God made man and woman with the command that they be fruitful and multiply (Genesis 1:26-29). Marriage is an institution for God's family to increase on earth.

God is multifaceted in His operations and He wants to express Himself in diverse dimensions on earth. The over 7 billion people on earth are different expressions of God, and He will keep manifesting His glory until His praise fills the whole earth. Your family is to show God's glory and nothing less.

God desires that earth will be an extension of heaven (Isaiah 66:1a, Matthew 6:10), and the best way to achieve His goal is the institution of marriage. Marriage is not just a coming together of two people. God's plan or intent is to cause His will to be done on earth, as it is in heaven (Luke 11:2). Through marriage, you invite God on earth. God dwells where love, peace, harmony and joy thrive. Whenever God sees a home that reflects such, He dwells there. Marriage is an invitation to bring God's glory and manifest presence to humanity.

The Bible says;

> *'And they heard the sound of the Lord God*
> *walking in the garden in the cool of the day,*
> *and Adam and his wife hid themselves from*
> *the presence of the Lord God among the*
> *trees of the garden.'*

GENESIS 3:8

God kept man in Eden, eastward of the Garden. To me, Eden was a symbolic representation of God's presence. But when the devil saw the marriage union's potential, he made Adam and Eve sin against God. Adam and Eve's sin caused them to *hide from the presence of the Lord God among the trees of the garden* and, eventually, to be cast out of Eden.

The devil introduced sin into the first family on earth to destroy God's intention for marriage. The devil still uses sin to attempt to corrupt marriage to this day. However, the family is always stronger when they hold hands together in prayers to God.

Dear husband and wife, you must keep your family stronger and established in God.

God wants to establish His kingdom on earth. It will only take a living unit of the family to sustain God's intention now and beyond.

The Two Shall Become One

*'That is why a man leaves his father
and mother and is united to his wife,
and they become one flesh.'*

GENESIS 2:24

The Word of God describes marriage as the coming together of a man and a woman as they unite to become one flesh. Marriage brings together two separate individuals of different lifestyles, characters, and backgrounds. Once married, a man and woman no longer remain two single individuals, but one flesh. However, this does not mean that the couple have lost their identities. It only means that God brought two unique people together to fulfil one goal on earth.

We first need to understand that God doesn't make mistakes. He joins two people together in holy matrimony to make something out of them. When you agree to join hands in marriage with another person, you shift the focus from 'I', 'me' and 'mine' to thoughts like 'you' and 'ours'.

Marriage is about building a formidable team that will align with the will of God and raise godly seed (Malachi 2:15) to destroy the works of the kingdom of darkness and bring glory and praise to God (Psalm 8:2, Matthew 21:16). Your partner is a vital part of you. As a result, caring for your partner is akin to caring for yourself. It would be unwise to take care of some parts of our body and neglect others. At some point, the neglected parts would suffer and cause the entire body to suffer. If you neglect to take care of your wife and instead only focus on yourself, then eventually, both of you will suffer.

After the fall of man in Eden, man became selfish and self-centred. As humans, we tend to be more concerned with our own happiness and comfort than that of others. This is why it is often said that 'marriage takes work'. A marriage requires understanding and intentional effort to put your partner above yourself and to put the marriage relationship above everything else.

A husband who is willing to build his home must understand that intimacy is not a one-day affair. We need to work at it. However, it does not take just one to be intimate but two. Below are some of the ways you can develop intimacy in marriage:

Emotional Intimacy

A husband and wife must be willing to open up emotionally to one another. Additionally, you should protect your partner's emotions. In a good marriage, each partner feels safe enough to open up about their personal feelings.

Physical Intimacy

There is nothing more binding than sexual intimacy in marriage. A couple becomes physically one through sex, just as God designed from the beginning. Physical intimacy should not be restricted to the bedroom. Couples must be intimate outside the bedroom as well. Things like holding hands, frequent hugs, romantic words, and outings together build physical intimacy in the marriage. A simple touch can communicate support, compassion, concern, appreciation, understanding and love.

Spiritual Intimacy

You might think that intimacy does not mix with spirituality. Some might say it is for the carnally minded. Contrary to this misconception, married couples are one in all areas—physically, emotionally, financially, etc.

Christ is at the centre of your marriage at all times. A healthy household is not just about you and what you want; it is creating room for Christ in your home. Spiritual intimacy is the foundation upon which other forms of intimacy are built. It is the spiritual that controls the physical. If your spiritual activity at home is intact, your home will be stable.

Activities like daily prayers, worship, devotions, and Bible study strengthen and unify the home, leaving no room for the devil. When striving for spiritual intimacy together, do not forget your personal relationship with God, which is as important as that with your spouse.

Performing daily activities together creates unity and harmony within a household; as the saying goes, *a family that prays together stays together*. The marital bond between a husband and wife is one of the strongest to keep the devil away. Togetherness makes your marriage a formidable force against the wiles of the enemy (Psalm 133:1).

As the husband, the more you confide in your wife about your job, business, and day-to-day affairs, the better your marriage. Not only is strength built in togetherness, but also is trust. One way to show that you have developed trust is by sharing problems, dreams and even ambitions with your spouse.

Your wife is your partner in all spheres. She is your best friend, lover, confidant, and everything you can ever imagine. You owe her all explanations about your past achievements and misdeeds, your present actions, and your future plans. Any woman you cannot trust is not fit to be your wife and vice versa. Developing trust within a marriage requires full disclosure with your spouse.

Do not hide anything. Keeping secrets in marriage is like a time bomb. It will explode eventually. Let your wife know who you are, inside-out, and you are sure to enjoy the bliss of a beautiful home.

THE PURPOSE OF MARRIAGE

Marriage is neither an escape from singlehood, a safe haven from poverty nor an avenue to wealth. Also, marriage does not shield you from the sin of fornication. Many people have turned marriage into what God never intended for it to be.

God's approach to marriage is quite different from any of the reasons mentioned above. In the beginning, God instituted marriage to provide man with what he needed: a companion, a helpmeet, and a way to create godly families on earth. Every other reason for marriage is built around these primary intentions:

Companionship

Humans are social beings. We need one another. There is nothing as beautiful as having a friend you can talk to about anything at any time. Companionship relieves burden and stress. God made mankind to relate with others. When He created Adam, He spoke with him as a man will talk with his friend but only periodically.

The Bible says:

> *'So Adam gave names to all cattle, to the birds of the air, and to every beast of the field. But for Adam there was not found a helper comparable to him.'*

GENESIS 2:20

Even though God made all animals, none could be a companion to Adam. Companionship is about people who understand each other, who readily share time with each, learn, and grow together: a role which an animal could not fill. Marriage was made for this purpose. As a husband, you are full of vitality, but still you face certain challenges that test your strength. In times of vulnerability, your wife and ultimate companion can strengthen you once again.

In life's journey, a companion keeps you strengthened more than when you are alone. God does not wish loneliness upon the children of His kingdom, so God designed marriage as the perfect platform for companionship.

Through bonding, we develop genuine companionship. Be one not only in your body, but also in faith, understanding, love and beliefs. Partners should be able to relate and talk about anything. You should be able to come into agreement on any issue. This will happen when both husband and wife can boldly say, 'my spouse is my best friend and my first partner.'

Helpmeet

Would you like to have someone to help you with your most challenging task? How about someone who can plan, think, and pull resources together with you? Marriage is the perfect place to find a person who relieves some of the physical and mental stresses in life.

Marriage was made for two with the sole aim of helping each other. Having someone to bear your burden with you is quite a relief and comfort. It makes life easier and worth fighting for. That was what God gave to Adam in Eden (Genesis 2:20). When God gave Adam a woman, God gave him a helper.

You need help as a husband. God has committed so much to you that you alone cannot actualise without the help of another. God made the woman in the similitude of the Holy Spirit. The Bible says:

> *'And I will pray to the Father, and He will*
> *give you another Helper, that He may abide*
> *with you forever — the Spirit of truth, whom*
> *the world cannot receive because it neither*
> *sees Him nor knows Him; but you know Him,*
> *for He dwells with you and will be in you.'*

JOHN 14:16

PARTNERS SHOULD BE ABLE TO RELATE AND TALK ABOUT ANYTHING

Awesome! The above text is Jesus's word to His disciples when He was about to leave the earth, after spending three and a half years with them. The Holy Spirit was the promise of a helper to the disciples.

Similarly, God gave Adam a woman as his helper (Genesis 2:20). When you consider the attributes of a good woman, you will realise many of her virtues are similar to that of the Holy Spirit. A wife gives comfort, encouragement, strength, and motivation to achieve God's assignment. She is the best counsellor when making decisions about your life, business, or career.

While the man has his roles to play in his wife's life, so has God made women to bear the dreams, carry the vision and support the divine call of her husband. God's design for the woman enables her to fulfil her divine mandate in marriage.

Admittedly, these are wonderful traits. However, the devil has seen it, and he knows that the woman is a significant force behind any successful man. So, the devil hijacks the woman's strength and turns it against her (Genesis 3:1-10).

It is impossible to enjoy the help of a woman who is not a child of God. This is why the Bible spoke clearly saying: *Do not be unequally yoked together with unbelievers. For what fellowship has righteousness with lawlessness? And what communion has light with darkness?* (2 Corinthians 6:14). The best marriage is Christian marriage, and nothing less.

Dear husband, you need a woman who understands her divine input in the marriage and is ready to put her life on the line for it.

Fellowshiping with God

'You are worthy, O Lord, to receive glory and honour and power; for You created all things, and by Your will, they exist and were created.'

REVELATION 4:11

Yes! In God's plan, marriage is a strategic institution. Nothing was created without God's consent. Therefore, everything God made must acknowledge the Creator. God does not need food or a house, nor does He demand anything from you except to worship Him. You will be surprised to know that your worship of God is one reason God made marriage.

In order to sustain continuous worship, God chose marriage to bring two people together, who will pass on the baton of worship from generation to generation. Your marriage is meant to glorify God.

God wants to see that homes on earth recognise His supremacy and acknowledge Him as God of all. Raise the altar of worship to God, and you will be surprised how He will move in your family and in every affair that concerns you.

Subsequently, other secondary purposes of marriage aside these three major reasons include:

Meeting your Needs

The truth of the matter is that God has provided everything you need to live a fulfilled life. The moment the scripture says that God rested from all His work that was it. Everything has been made available for you. Sometimes, people ask God for what He has already given them. The Bible says:

'As His divine power has given to us all things that pertain to life and godliness, through the knowledge of Him who called us by glory and virtue, by which have been given to us exceedingly great and precious promises, that through these you may be partakers of the divine nature...'

2 PETER 1:3-4

You do not lack anything. Why, then, do you feel as if you do not have what you need? The answer is simple: searching in the wrong places. Often, we look in the wrong place for help. One of the best places to find help is within your marriage.

The institution of marriage is designed to meet each other's needs. God made the husband to meet the needs of the wife and vice versa. However, a couple must understand each other's needs to enjoy the marriage.

The greatest need of a man is not sex! Though a man needs sexual intimacy with his wife, a man's greatest need is respect, especially from his wife. He may look for respect in his workplace, gym or church. But none compares to the respect given to him at home by his wife. When a woman gives her husband respect in her actions and words, it makes a happy husband and marriage.

The most significant need of a woman is not new clothes or fashionable shoes. Instead, a woman needs security most from a man. A woman feels loved when she is emotionally, physically, financially and spiritually secured in the relationship. When a man strives to make his spouse feel secure, he demonstrates his love for her. Security will result in contentment and happiness. And remember, a happy wife makes a happy home.

You must understand that both husband and wife have the power to influence the relationship. You can use this power for good, which brings progress in the home, or for selfish desires which can destroy the marriage. Choosing to positively influence your household will allow both of you enjoy a home that exemplifies heaven on earth.

Intended for Pleasure

Of course, marriage is for sexual pleasure. This should not surprise you because God gave this natural craving to all. However, sex must be practiced within the right context, which is marriage. The moment you begin to feel a consistent drive for sex as a mature man, then it's high time you get married to avoid the sin of sexual immorality.

> 'Marriage is honourable among all,
> and the bed undefiled, but fornicators
> and adulterers God will judge.'
>
> HEBREWS 13:4

Sex is best enjoyed in marriage. Any form of sexual activity outside marriage is an abuse of the gift of sex. Sexual intimacy in marriage is the most intimate expression of love between a man and a woman. God designed it to fulfil our need for receiving and expressing love. Besides the pleasure you derive from sex in marriage, it is also for childbearing.

Marriage is for Childbearing

> 'Then God blessed them, and God
> said to them, 'Be fruitful and multiply;
> fill the earth and subdue it...'
>
> GENESIS 1:28A

God made marriage to be a place where you can raise godly children who will live for God and establish His kingdom here on earth. Your children will imitate the life you show to them. If you want them to live for God, then lead them to the cross because no one comes to the Father except through Jesus.

Marriage is a home where you build your children to have a relationship with God, and they can pass it on to their children's children.

God has entrusted nations into your hands as couples, and you must not fail in your assignment!.

Make the most of every opportunity you have to fellowship with God, and you will notice clear changes in your outlook, your perspective and how you relate with your family. Words cannot describe the joy that exudes from fellowship with God.

Therefore, precious wife, fill up the fellowship space if it is lacking. And if you've been there before, do ensure to always stay in God's presence. When you do, your words will carry power and grace, and the fruit of the Holy Spirit will be evident in you. Remember, you have a ministry in God's presence.

3

GOD'S MIND
FOR HIM

CHAPTER THREE

God's Mind for Him

God is not an abstract being. Many assume God is inaccessible, cannot be seen, or talked with. None of these myths about God is true. Our God is almighty, yet He comes to interact with humanity as seen in Genesis 3:8 and several other verses in the Bible. The Bible tells us that Adam and Eve heard the voice of God in the garden. Now consider this, if He is mysterious, how do you think anyone could hear His voice? Not only did God speak to them in the garden, but He also checked on their wellbeing when He asked: "Where are you?" (Genesis 3:9).

So, God has a mouth to speak, a listening ear and a heart that cares. You should never assume that God cannot feel neither your suffering nor understand the challenges around your life. The Bible confirms that God came to earth in the nature of man to relate to what humanity feels. He experienced all the human feelings ever-present in natural man. He was humiliated, disgraced, celebrated, tortured, loved and betrayed. The Bible says:

"Who, being in the form of God, did not consider it robbery to be equal with God, but made Himself of no reputation, taking the form of a bondservant, and coming in the likeness of men."

PHILIPPIANS 2:6-7

This passage implies that God became man to know how pain, sorrow, anger, bitterness, joy and other emotions feel in the human flesh. Nonetheless, none of these human emotions are strange to God because we all came from Him. You are made in the image and likeness of God. God is your Father, and you are His child. Nothing about you is strange to God.

The image of God (imago dei) in man refers to the immaterial part of humanity. It sets human beings apart from the animal world, fits us for the dominion God intended us to have over the earth (Genesis 1:28), and enables us to commune with our Maker. It is a mental, moral, and social likeness.

Mentally, human beings can reason and choose. This is a reflection of God's intellect and freedom. Anytime someone invents a machine, writes a book, paints a landscape, enjoys a symphony, calculates a sum, or names a pet, he or she is proclaiming the fact that we are made in God's image.

Morally, humanity was created in righteousness and perfect innocence, a reflection of God's holiness. God saw all He had made (humanity included) and called it "very good" (Genesis 1:31). Our conscience is a vestige of that original state. Whenever someone writes a law, recoils from evil, praises good behaviour, or feels guilty, he or she is confirming the fact that we are made in God's own image.

Socially, humanity was created for fellowship. This reflects God's triune nature and His love. In Eden, humanity's primary relationship was with God (Genesis 3:8 implies fellowship with God), and God made the first woman because "it is not good for the man to be alone" (Genesis 2:18). Every time someone marries, makes a friend, hugs a child, or attends church, he or she is demonstrating the fact that we are made in the likeness of God.

Beloved…, you are who you are because God thought it first in His heart to make a man in His image and likeness. Before you were born, God had already defined your purpose and assignment on earth. You are neither an accident nor a mistake regardless of how your birth came about. When God created Adam as a man, what God saw was nations flowing from a single man. He foresaw that through one man, many great people would be born.

God called Abraham the father of many nations (Genesis 17:4) even before Abraham had a single child. So, why would God call Abraham a father, a man who had no children yet? What does fatherhood entail? Can you differentiate between fatherhood and being a husband? What is God's mind for every man? We hope you will find answers to these questions in this chapter of *the Ministry of the Husband*.

GOD'S MIND FOR YOU

> *"Then God said, "Let Us make man in our image, according to Our likeness; let them have dominion over the fish of the sea, over the birds of the air, and over the cattle, over all the earth and over every creeping thing that creeps on the earth."*
>
> GENESIS 1:26

There was something in the mind of God when He created the man, Adam. God's purpose for Adam was already established before creation. God needed someone who would be like Him and legislate on His behalf on earth just as He is in heaven. The Almighty God created an extension of heaven on earth and someone had to have His traits to oversee the affairs on earth. So, God made man. Every man is God's representative born with a leadership trait, management ability and a heart full of love.

Per his design, the man is built with physical and mental strength to bear the weight of others and not to be a bully or to abuse women. Man is created to lead the frontier of the family to cause advancement and national development. As a man, you lead while others follow. But without God who made you like Him, how will you know the direction to lead others? This is why it is dangerous for any woman to commit to a covenant of marriage with a man who is not led by God.

God made men be like Himself in all facets of life. Man looks like God in all respects. He is an extension of God on earth. God is a father, and He made all men be fathers too. Therefore, every boy is potentially a father. Fatherhood has nothing to do with childbearing but an understanding of your purpose and assignment in the family, society, church and everywhere you find yourself as a man. The role of a man is summed up in one, and that is fatherhood. Fathers are representatives of God. You represent God as a source, sustainer, protector, leader, and husband.

The father as a source

God created all things. This means that He is the source of all things. Everything you see today, visible or invisible was first conceived inside of God before it materialised. You are a father because of your ability to make possible for others what they cannot do for themselves. As a father, lives depend on you, and you must never fail them. A source supplies and also sustains.

The father as a sustainer

First, God made man out of dust. But man would not have lasted without a means of surviving. So, God breathed into man, and he became a living soul (Genesis 2:7). God's breath is the sustainer of the earthly man's life. Likewise, as a father, you are not only a source; you also sustain what proceeds out of you. You may bring forth a child but being able to provide for the needs of the child is what makes you a sustainer.

The father as a protector

God is our heavenly Father who protects us from evil. Since men are fathers on earth, their physical muscles enable them to protect the vulnerable. As a man, you work with your physical and mental strength to protect your family from the scourge of poverty, oppression and bullies.

The father as a leader

A leading father is God's kind of man. In the home, leadership is hierarchical. You must allow God to lead you as a father so that you can lead others well. Any man who leads without following God's leadership will soon land himself in trouble and may find no one to rescue him. Your leadership role is to stand as a mediator between God and your family or society. Jesus said:

> "Most assuredly, I say to you, the Son
> can do nothing of Himself, but what He
> sees the Father do; for whatever He does,
> the Son also does in like manner."
>
> JOHN 5:19

The father's role is a spiritual assignment. You cannot solve a spiritual problem by human reasoning. You need a higher authority for guidance. For others to follow you as a father, you must follow God first.

THE HUSBAND ROLE

Any man who is in a covenant union with a woman is a husband. Marriage is a call for a man to step up into His fatherly role as a husband. Whether the marriage results in childbearing or not, your fatherly role is not affected nor rendered invalid. Childbearing is not the only responsibility for a husband. When God created man, lovemaking was not what came first. God made man physically stronger than the woman (1 Peter 3:7 AMPC) to enable him shoulder responsibilities and defend his family. So, becoming a husband is not only for procreation.

"The Lord God planted a garden eastward in Eden, and there He put the man whom He had formed."

GENESIS 2:8

God placed man in the middle of all that He had created to manage it. This means a husband is first responsible for his family, managing his home, and caring for his wife as though she were his child, even before childbearing. As a husband, you are a father to your wife. You don't need to wait until you start having children before you carry out this duty. Therefore, child-bearing is an extension of your fatherhood responsibilities within the family. A husband is a father with the sacred duty to lead, guide, and manage his home.

Adam's fatherly role started before God brought Eve to him. He was taking care of all that God had already made in the Garden of Eden: he was naming the animals and taking care of the Garden (Genesis 2:15). But when God brought Eve, Adam became not only a father to Eve but also her husband. He saw Eve and recognised that she was a part of him. As a husband, you must learn to recognise the potential your wife carries. Women are an upgraded version of men according to the Bible.

The Bible says Adam was made from the dust (Genesis 2:7). However, his wife, Eve, was not made from the dust but from the rib of Adam (Genesis 2:22), an indication that your wife is the physical manifestation of who you are mentally, emotionally, and more.

The woman has a womb not only with the capacity to carry babies but also to conceive great ideas. If you make her feel less relevant, those ideas that should make you and the family great will not materialise. As a husband, you must learn to allow your wife deliver safely, the great ideas she carries in her womb. The raw material for your greatness is in your wife but until you help her process it well and fertilise it with your love, care and fatherly role in her life, those raw materials might remain dormant in her.

THE PROVIDER

By divine design, the husband is the giver in the home. He gives his sperm, and the wife receives it and produces a baby. A wife is a woman with a womb. The woman processes the sperm in her womb into something unique, and a child is born.

What you make available in your home, is multiplied later. You cannot keep giving your wife insults, abuse and expect her to bring forth something good out of it. It is garbage in, garbage out. The husband provides, and his wife multiplies what he gives. You do not need to be the wealthiest to be a provider. Being the provider is your responsibility to your family, and you must do it diligently.

> *"But if anyone does not provide for his own,*
> *and especially for those of his household,*
> *he has denied the faith and is worse than*
> *an unbeliever."*
>
> 1 TIMOTHY 5:8

As a husband, your responsibility is to provide in multiple aspects of family life. It transcends providing money for the family. Of course, you should provide for the family's financial needs; but moreso, you must provide emotional, spiritual, and mental support within the home. As a husband, providing love to your family will foster happiness and keep your family together.

Emotional Support

Most times, some husbands find it difficult to provide emotional support for their wives. You must understand that, by nature, a woman is particularly emotional. When she is happy, the home will be in a good state. Her joy spills over to her children and everything within the home. On the other hand, when she is sad, everything else will seem to fall out of place in the home. Therefore, her husband must always provide the emotional support she needs.

> *"Then Elkanah, her (Hannah) husband, said to her, "Hannah, why do you weep? Why do you not eat? And why is your heart grieved? Am I not better to you than ten sons?"*

I SAMUEL 1:8

An example of emotional support is seen in this case. Elkanah her husband spoke words of hope, encouragement and comfort to Hannah anytime she was upset. He never allowed his ego to get in his way when it came to providing emotional support for his wife. The story of Elkanah and Hannah is an essential lesson for every husband. Your wife needs you most in times of hardship. Keeping your wife comfortable and happy will solve many household problems.

Spiritual Wellbeing

It is your responsibility as a Christian husband to provide an altar of fellowship in the home. The husband presents God to his wife and children. He also ensures they uphold the spiritual tenets of the home. The husband is the spiritual head in the home and must provide for the family's spiritual needs. You feed your family with God's

Word. It is dangerous for a family if the man of the house cannot hear from God. The purpose of a Christian home was revealed in the Bible right from the beginning.

"And the Lord God commanded the man, saying, "Of every tree of the garden you may freely eat; but of the tree of the knowledge of good and evil you shall not eat, for in the day that you eat of it you shall surely die."

GENESIS 2:16-17

The man hears divine instruction and must be able to communicate it accurately to his family. This is what it means to be the provider of spiritual wellbeing in the home. You must have a good connection with God as a husband. You receive from God and make what you receive available for your home. As a result, there will be no spiritual provision in the home if the man has no spiritual connection with God.

God gave Joseph (the husband) instruction about his wife Mary (Matthew 1:18-25). God reaffirmed His promises to Abraham (the husband) about his children and generations yet to be born (Genesis 11). Job (the husband) was the man always making sacrifices for His children (Job 1:1-5). All these men were husbands, had a relationship with God and could hear God's instructions about their wives and family. God could do nothing without telling the priest of the home. As a husband, you are the priest, and you must always provide the sacrifice of incense on your family altar.

"He has shown you, O man, what is good;
And what does the Lord require of you but
to do justly, to love mercy, and to walk
humbly with your God?"

MICAH 6:8

Amazing! Every husband needs to see himself in the light of God's Word. True masculinity is humility before God. Faith demonstrated in humility is received from God. This is what God requires from the husband. You gain more respect and honour in your home when you humble yourself before God. You see, it is not about what you desire to have as a man but what you are ready to forgo. Let go of your ego and submit to God, and you will see how much God will make Himself available for you and your family.

God told Abraham to walk perfectly before Him (Genesis 17:1). This was actually not

> **IT IS DANGEROUS FOR A FAMILY IF THE MAN OF THE HOUSE CANNOT HEAR FROM GOD**

for Abraham's sake but for what God would do in his family and lineage. If you want to see God in your home as a husband, then you have to submit to God, and He will make Himself available in your home.

The Financier

Inarguably, the husband is the main financier of the home. You are not only a father and a source; you are also a sustainer. Your job is to sustain the family, your wife and your children. As a father and a husband, money is a significant means if you are to be responsible for your family's needs. Being able to meet your wife's financial demands indicates how much you care, respect and honour her. She might earn more than you, but that does not take away your responsibility as a provider. Although your wife might choose to support the home financially, you must be the provider in the home. When you do not have enough, communicate it well to your family and then go the extra mile to provide for the home. A good man will do everything legitimately possible to provide for his home.

A husband who does not have a job or shifts from one job to another and is not ready to take the responsibility of a provider would fall victim to low self-esteem. In an attempt to justify his irresponsibility, such a man will do everything to drag his family into the same pit of low-esteem so that he can 'feel' like a man in the home. Being a husband is not a feeling: taking responsibility for the home is what makes you a husband. A husband creates insecurity in his wife and children when he can't provide for their needs. Never abandon your family's financial needs.

Take care of your wife the same way you will take care of your babies even before you have any. Like I said, a husband is like a father to his wife. You have the responsibility to feed her, clothe her, protect her, counsel her and provide for her needs.

THE 'HOUSE-BAND'

The word 'husband' did not refer to a married man when it was first used in the first millennium. The original word means *the head of the house*. He could be married, single, or divorced. Over time, the word husband evolved. Since the men who were made head of households were married men, the word husband became the term used to describe the man who banded the house together. Hence, the husband came to be as the house-band.

A husband binds and connects the family. You must keep your house together and in order, just as a band binds a sheaf of wheat. Not all married men are husbands. The reason for this is not far-fetched. A married man who cannot keep his home together in unity or support the family is not fit to be called a husband. In such a home, the wife who shoulders the burden of family, works assiduously to feed the home, and does all she can to hold the family together is, in turn, the husband.

Never allow your position in the home to be given to another. Responsibility defines your role as a husband. The wife has her role in the home, and you have yours too. While your assignment is to band the house together, your wife weaves the family together like threads of fabrics laced together to form a cloth. Homemaking is like weaving and providing support for the man who bands the home together. So, being a husband requires the cooperation of your wife and the children. Bonding your house together, must be a joint effort.

Consequently, the family is like a business corporation where the husband is the president, the mother, his vice, and the children, the board members. As the president of the home, you do not dictate or control. You must preside. The president of any corporation that would thrive well will never impose his opinion on his vice or board members. The president seeks their consent before deciding on any course of action. This is precisely how the husband ought to preside in the home. You do not act as a husband without getting advice from your wife. Aside from the physical differences between a man and a woman, both sexes possess an additional uniqueness. Whatever a man's weakness is, his wife has strength in that area. So, do not be a foolish husband who is a 'know-it-all'.

The Bible says:

> *"And if anyone thinks that he knows anything,*
> *he knows nothing yet as he ought to know."*
>
> 1 CORINTHIANS 8:2

You are not the Island of Knowledge. Seek counsel from your wife. She is the other half of you. A woman by design uses words better and wields soft power capable of changing situations and decisions. The children, who are the home's board members, are not left out in the family's decision-making. You must not be too busy to yield to the cry of your child. Your child needs you in what is most important to him or her. Plan your schedule in such a way that it will give room for time with the children too.

Always let your children know what you are doing while you are engaged in that venture or activity. Children are inquisitive and so open to learning. Share with them information about your job, why you come home late sometimes, the reason for relocation, why you could not attend games with them and lots more. Such information binds the home and gives the children a sense of belonging.

Boost your children's confidence by taking out time to chat with them on important issues of life or questions bothering their minds. Being hard on children is not the way to be a father or husband. I do not mean you should take every one of your children's matters with leniency.

The Bible affirms that he who spares his rod hates his son, but he who loves him disciplines him promptly (Proverbs 13:24). This implies that discipline is part of the way you parent a child, as a father. Teach them the difference between right and wrong without any form of physical abuse. Many people misinterpret this part of the scriptures as beating a child. This is a wrong interpretation of Bible truth. The 'rod' used in the Bible, as mentioned in the above verse is a metaphor. The biblically recommended way to discipline a child is to raise the child in the way he should go (not your way) (Proverbs 22:6). Remember, you are like a guardian to your child as a husband. Guide and do not enforce your will.

THE HOME MANAGER

"This is a faithful saying: If a man desires the position of a bishop, he desires a good work... One who rules his own house well, having his children in submission with all reverence (for if a man does not know how to rule

his own house, how will he take care of
the church of God)?"

1 TIMOTHY 3:1, 4-5

Management of the home is the greatest test of a man's leadership. If you will lead as a man in any capacity, your leadership skills must first be expressed in your family. Any Christian husband who wants to be a church leader must first manage his home well. Your family is your first ministry, and you must not fail here.

Often, some husbands spend more time counselling other men's wives than they spend with their own wives. Such husbands also tend to discipline other couples' children while they are unable to handle their home well. This contradicts who God made the husband to be. Your time with your family must be your top priority so learn to prioritise the people and occasions around your life.

> **MANAGEMENT OF THE HOME IS THE GREATEST TEST OF A MAN'S LEADERSHIP**

Your leadership in the home is perfected as a man when you can pass on the baton to the next generation. What legacy do you envision for your children after you are gone? What will your family remember you for? What have you done to ensure they

know how to manage a home? Can you sincerely answer these questions yourself?

A good man leaves an inheritance for his children (Proverbs 13:22). Putting the family in debt is not an excellent way to manage the home. Live within your means and learn to differentiate between what is needed and what is desired within the home. Be an example of a good leader to your wife and children.

Dear husband, your family is your most sacred responsibility. It is a divine assignment. Once a man fails in the home, such a man has failed in life. You own the key to lock and unlock the potentials of everyone within your home. Therefore, you must know how to wield this power well. Every other role as a husband in the home rests on one peculiar duty: being the priest of the home. Being a priest is your only spiritual duty to your family on which other responsibilities revolve or hinge. Stand in your place and never compromise. In the next chapter, we shall be discussing the role of the husband as a priest exclusively.

4

HUSBAND
- THE PRIEST

CHAPTER FOUR

Husband
- the Priest

*'Husbands, love your wives,
just as Christ also loved the church
and gave Himself for her.'*

EPHESIANS 5:25

Why was the husband commanded to love his wife like Christ loved the church? How did Christ love the church? What type of love does Christ have for the church? Does love mean dying for your lover? Now let's delve further into the Bible text.

First, I would like to clarify that Christ was not Jesus's last name or another name by which he was known. The name Christ was a title given to Jesus, and it means the 'anointed one'. Jesus is the anointed one. He is the anchor upon which the Church stands victorious. Of course, there will be no Church without the anointed one (Jesus Christ).

The Church is the body while Jesus Christ is the head. Now, how would you think the body will survive without the head? The head is the leading figure. Wherever the head turns, the body follows. Jesus Christ is the arrowhead of the Church, through whom the church has access to God. However, it was the sacrifice Christ made that gave this access to the church.

The Bible says:

> *'So also Christ did not glorify Himself to become High Priest, but it was He (God) who said to Him: 'You are My Son, today I have begotten you.' He also says in another place: 'You are a priest forever according to the order of Melchizedek.'*
>
> HEBREWS 5:5-6

The love of Jesus and His sacrifice for mankind grants Him the eternal Priestly office. Therefore, any man who wants to step into the priestly office of a husband must first understand the priesthood of Jesus Christ. Jesus's death on the cross was an act of His love. Similarly, husbands must love their wives sacrificially as priest of the home, standing in the gap for the family.

THE PRIESTHOOD OF THE BELIEVER

The priesthood of Jesus gives us insight into the priestly office of every husband in the home. Let us take our study from the beginning of man's creation. As you would have seen in previous chapters, God created the man first and placed him in the garden. God's intention has always been that man mirrors the kingdom of God and establish it on earth.

In the New Testament, the Bible tells us that we are heirs of God and joint-heirs with Christ – '...*and if children, then heirs—heirs of God and joint-heirs with Christ, if indeed we suffer with Him, that we may also be glorified together.*' (Romans 8:17). This is a spiritual reality for every believer. You have access to God just the same way any other believer does. When Christ died, the veil in the temple tore apart, and it paved the way for ALL to have direct access to God through Him with whom we are joint heirs.

Jesus Christ, through His death, burial and resurrection, reconciled us all to God (Romans 5:10, 2 Corinthians 5:18). Whether male or female, Jew or Gentile, you are a son of God through faith in Christ Jesus (Galatians 3:27-28). So, according to our new birth in the Spirit, every child of God is a priest. Every one of us has access to the Father. We can all enter into the holy places and offer up incense and sacrifices unto our God as priests.

So, what happens during marital unification? Does God instruct the husband to be the priest in his home?

Remember, in the introductory part of this chapter, we started with Ephesians 5:25, which says, *'Husbands, love your wives, just as Christ also loved the church and gave Himself for her.'* This Bible text compares the husband's position and responsibility in the home to that of Jesus Christ and the church. This implies that man represents, in the natural, what Christ represents in the spiritual. .

As a student of the scriptures, you will understand that Christ taught His followers using earthly things to make comparisons with deep spiritual concepts for their understanding. God uses types and shadows by using physical things to represent eternal realities. One of the reasons for this is that you may comprehend the spiritual truth by seeing the heavenly realities through the lens of earthly concepts. In other words, as a husband, you have a spiritual responsibility in the physical realm which Christ operated in while He was on earth.

Jesus, being God in the body of man, would discern what God wanted to do and carried them out in a manner that those around him could relate with.

The Bible says:

'Then Jesus answered and said to them,
Most assuredly, I say to you, the Son can
do nothing of Himself, but what He sees
the Father do; for whatever He does,
the Son also does in like manner.'

JOHN 5:19

Jesus, therefore, would in many of His teachings liken the kingdom of God to events around Him so that the people could relate with those spiritual realities. By so doing, Jesus Christ revealed God to the people. He was the mediator and priest on behalf of the people. Similarly, the husband needs to show God to his family. He should hear God for them and bring God closer to them. Often, you need to get your family to the point that you let them see God for themselves in all that happens within the home.

> **HUSBANDS MUST LOVE THEIR WIVES SACRIFICIALLY AS PRIEST OF THE HOME**

Subsequently, our focus in this part of the book will be on *Jesus Christ's words*. We will consider the priestly role of Christ then and now, and what we are expected to learn and do as a husband.

As a husband, the standard for your role in marriage is *Christ*. Every child of God is a priest unto God. Nevertheless, husbands are called to play a unique priestly role in the family context. As a husband, you are God's representative to your family, and you must present yourself well. Although both husband and wife have access to being the priest in the home, priestly leadership will be missing if the husband does not step into his ministry.

The Priest on Duty

'And these are the names of the sons of Aaron: Nadab, the firstborn, and Abihu, Eleazar, and Ithamar. These are the names of the sons of Aaron, the anointed priests, whom he consecrated to minister as priests.'

NUMBERS 3:2-3

In the Old Testament, only one priest had access to the Holy of Holies - the High Priest. Even though there were many other priests present, the High Priest was the only one who made the sacrifice. Consider the four sons of Aaron in the Old Testament. These were all priests unto God, but they did not always perform their priestly roles at the same time.

However, this does not change the fact that the four sons of Aaron were all priests. When one of them was designated to perform the priesthood duties at a specific time, the other priests would wait on him. The one performing the priestly role was the priest on duty. Likewise, the husband is the priest on duty in the home.

ABIDING IN HIS PRESENCE

In the Old Testament, only the High Priest went into the Holy of Holies. This happened once a year. The High Priest went before God to make atonement for the sin of the people. In the Holy of Holies was the Ark of the Covenant, which was a figurative representation of the Presence of God (Exodus 40).

Now, this is what the Priest did as part of his duty: He sprinkled the blood of the lamb on the Ark of the Covenant. The sprinkling of blood brought redemption, provision, and forgiveness to the people. However, this happened only when the High Priest entered the Holy of Holies—the Dwelling place of the Presence of God.

If a priest casually entered the Presence of God, the consequences were always severe. Nadab and Abihu, Aaron's sons, are examples of priests who did not regard God's Presence. They thought they could approach God's Presence anyhow. As a result, they perished (Leviticus 10:2). From the outer court into the inner courts, there was a purification right for priests to ensure they did not enter the Presence of God unclean.

*No man of the descendants of Aaron the
Priest, who has a defect, shall come near to
offer the offerings made by fire to the Lord. He
has a defect; he shall not come near to offer
the bread of his God. He may eat the bread of
his God, both the holiest and the holy; only he
shall not go near the veil or approach the altar
because he has a defect, lest he profane My
sanctuaries; for I the Lord sanctify them.*

LEVITICUS 21:21-23

In other words, priests are men in God's Presence. You cannot function in the priesthood office outside God's Presence.

Dear husband, your first call as a priest over your family is to be acquainted with the Presence of God. That is where your ministry as a husband begins.

SPEND TIME IN GOD'S PRESENCE

Do you aspire to lead your home well? What do you desire for your family? Do you seek to bring your children to God's knowledge? Then, you must be a man who dwells in God's Presence. Every man who aspires to lead his home well must learn how to spend time alone in God's Presence. This is essential because it is where man finds meaning for existence. He understands his purpose and his place in God's eternal agenda when he finds himself in the Presence of God—through a consistent lifestyle of worship, prayer and the study of the Word of God.

The Presence – Man's Habitation

God placed Adam in Eden. The purpose was simple; as long as Adam stayed in Eden, he would live forever and work in God's purpose for his life. Like I mentioned earlier, to me, Eden was never a physical location but the Presence of God (Genesis 2:8).

However, God planted a garden not too far from Eden: a symbolic representation of the Presence of God and the home.

The Bible says:

> *'Now a river went out of Eden to*
> *water the garden...'*
>
> GENESIS 2:10

The resources your family needs flow from your continual stay in the Presence of God. Never leave God's Presence. It is in God's Presence you enjoy divine supply for your home, and nowhere else.

You will also realise that after man sinned, God drove him and his wife out of Eden. The implication was that man no longer was privy to the Presence of God. He began to struggle and toil laboriously (**Genesis 3**).

God wanted man to enjoy a deeper dimension of fellowship, more than he had experienced in Eden. Therefore, God placed the new man *in Christ*. Also, this is neither a physical geographical location. It is a spiritual reality that does not need logic or reasoning but faith. God knew that it is only in Christ that man can access His Presence without any kind of sacrifice or ritual. So, all you have to do is in one of Apostle Peter's messages:

> *Repent therefore and be converted,*
> *that your sins may be blotted out,*
> *so that times of refreshing may come*
> *from the Presence of the Lord...*
>
> ACTS 3:19

Are you experiencing struggles in your family, career, or business? Do you do so much but get little out of your labour? Are you in doubt of your choices and decisions, and has confusion taken over your heart? Regardless of the moment, you need to retrace your steps back to God's Presence. Nothing happens on earth without a spiritual backup. Likewise, nothing will change in your home if you do not rise to your duty as the spiritual man of the home.

Husbands who continue to live like carnal men when they have a supernatural heritage will end up leading their family into a life of misery and turmoil. The only way out of such misery is a decision to follow God's Presence.

Repent and return to God. Once you do that, you will begin to enjoy endless moments of refreshment from the Presence of God. You will make decisions with ease and accuracy and take bold steps on new projects because your source of inspiration is God's Presence. Moreover, you will be able to lead your family through moments of need because of the strength and wisdom you received by spending quality time with God.

There was never a time when Jesus was confused. He knew what to say at any point in time. He understood what to do in every situation, and He never made a mistake. Have you tried to ponder on what could have been His secret? Of course, it was the Presence of God. There were several instances that the Bible recorded that Jesus got up early in the morning to spend time with the Father (Luke 5:16)

Jesus was constantly in touch with God the Father while He was on earth. He never did anything without the Father's consent. Jesus was always in the Presence of God.

The Evidence of His Presence

Now, I want to clearly show to you husbands that it is possible to go about your daily activities and remain in the Presence of God. Yes! Jesus lived such an exemplary life in the Spirit. He showed us that the Presence of God is not a fixed location or a geographical area. The Presence of God is found within us.

The Bible says:

> *'Most assuredly, I say to you, he who hears*
> *My word and believes in Him who sent Me*
> *has everlasting life, and shall not come into*
> *judgment, but has passed from death into*
> *life...For as the Father has life in Himself,*
> *so He has granted the Son to have life in*
> *Himself...'*
>
> JOHN 5:24-26

God is with you the very moment you receive Christ into your heart. Just as I rightly said, God's Presence is only accessed by faith. What we receive at salvation is the life of God— Zoe (Dzo'ay) which is "the real or genuine quality of life". No one gets the life of God and becomes threatened by situations around him. Zoe lives inside you, and His Spirit is real in you (John 14:16-18).

Practise God's Presence

You now understand that the Presence of God is with you, and His Spirit is in you. Therefore, you need to begin to practise God's Presence. Many husbands or Christians do not know that a person can practise the Presence of God with every action. The Presence of God does not indicate that you have the propensity for healing, miracles, deliverance unless you practise. Let me share with you the story of a man who continually practised God's Presence in his time.

Brother Lawrence was one of the ancient fathers of the faith who lived in the early seventeenth century. He wrote a book about the art of practising the Presence of God. In that book, Brother Lawrence documented his experiences of how he practised God's Presence everywhere he went. Even while he was doing the dishes at his place of work, he practised the Presence of God because he believed he carried God's Presence within him.

The people who worked with Brother Lawrence testified that there was usually a form of brightness and glory that emanated from him whenever they saw him. Yes! That is the benefit of staying in the Presence of God all day—glory!

Brother Lawrence experienced boundless joy and peace in all seasons of his life due to his constant practice of God's

Presence. This can also be seen in the life and ministry of Jesus. The Bible recorded that Jesus remained peaceful amid a fierce storm.

> *"And suddenly, a great tempest arose*
> *on the sea so that the boat was covered*
> *with the waves. But He was asleep."*
>
> MATTHEW 8:24

This is fascinating. How could Jesus be sleeping amid that ferocious storm? He had an assurance that God was with Him. Therefore, He had no reason to be fearful. You cannot continue to live your life in fear—fear of death, fear of debt, fear of sickness, etc. Those who live in the Presence of God feel a resounding sense of peace and security.

IT IS IN GOD'S PRESENCE YOU ENJOY DIVINE SUPPLY FOR YOUR HOME

As a husband, you cannot successfully lead your wife when you live in abject fear. Therefore, never allow fear to rule your heart. Fear will put your home in jeopardy and it is a strong force that holds a home down. It first goes for the head of the home. Remember what the Bible says, "Strike the shepherd, and the sheep will scatter" (Zechariah 13:7). Do not allow fear to destroy your home. Be a man who dwells in His Presence, and fear will flee from you.

Do you remember that as long as Adam remained in the Presence of God (Eden), the glory of God was his covering? He was never naked. Also, do not forget that Moses spent forty days and nights on the mountain. All the while, he was in God's Presence. When he returned to the camp of the Israelites, he radiated brightness that the Israelites could not gaze upon without covering their faces. That was the glory of God (Exodus 34:29)! Jesus's transformation while he was spending time in God's Presence are some of the amazing benefits of practising God's Presence (Luke 9:28-29).

You can experience this glory in your marriage too by learning to be deliberate about God's Presence. Practising the Presence of God does not need to be during personal devotions only. When you are busy, be conscious of God. Speak His word under your breath through frequent meditation. Let your thoughts be on God at all times (Philippians 4:6). Speak to God and listen to Him as He speaks to your heart. All these are some of the ways you can practise the Presence of God. Right now, you can begin to cultivate God's Presence.

You need to pay attention to the Spirit of God in you and consciously engage Him all day as if you can see Him with your physical eyes. Over time, His Presence will become real to you—just practise. The truth of the matter is that you might experience some setbacks in this practice, but do not quit. Keep on practising God's Presence, and in no time, you will see Him evident in your life and in your home.

Lead your Family into His Presence

"But I want you to know that the head of every man is Christ, the head of the woman is man, and the head of Christ is God."

1 CORINTHIANS 11:3

Your first ministry as the priest in your home is to lead your family into God's Presence continually. After realising that the Presence of God is not restricted to a location, know that you can enjoy God's Presence at all times in all places. Do this, and every member of your family will learn to live in God's Presence even when you are not with them.

Jesus had the habit of taking His disciples to the mountain to spend time together with them. Most times, they talked about the things of the kingdom of God. Jesus led His disciples to God's Presence because He knew a time would come when He would not be with them.

The disciples needed to learn how to do the things He did and even greater things in His absence through the help of the Holy Spirit who would come to live in them. They needed to replicate His life here on earth after His departure. So, the best thing Jesus could do was to keep leading them into God's Presence, the source of His strength.

One of such occasions was documented in the gospels thus:

> *Now after six days Jesus took Peter,*
> *James, and John his brother, led them*
> *up on a high mountain by themselves...*
>
> MATTHEW 17:1

The latter parts of the New Testament books show that these three disciples who were always with Jesus became the pillars of the first church. They provided the godly leadership needed for the church after Jesus left the earth.

Dear husband, your wife and children can know God intimately if you relentlessly lead them into God's Presence. They can also become instruments in God's hand to influence many other people to come to the Lord, and your family can become a model in the body of Christ. First, you need to stand up to your duty as the priest in the home.

Beloved brother, your success or failure as a husband lies in how much you know the Presence of God and how much you abide in it. Life becomes more meaningful when you know the Presence of God and live in it the rest of your life.

THE PRAYING PRIEST

The priesthood is a role that demands a total consecration and commitment. It is a ministry you must not take with levity. Earlier in this chapter, we established the place of the husband as the priest in his home. Now, we will look at some of the responsibilities of a priest and how they relate the role of a husband in the family.

> *"Then He spoke a parable to them that*
> *men always ought to pray and not lose heart."*
>
> LUKE 18:1

One of the fundamental duties of a priest is prayer. Every priest has a call to commune with God on behalf of the people he represents. For a priest, prayer is not just an obligation; it is devotion and a ministry on its own. Every husband must see it as a lifetime commitment.

Prayer is what makes things happen. Every change and transformation you desire rises and falls on prayer. If an institution like marriage can survive in this ever-changing society, prayer must become something you devote yourself to. Hence, prayer is the oxygen that keeps the family alive. A prayerless family becomes prey to the enemy.

Communion

The priest goes into the Presence of God bearing his needs and those of the people in his care. He goes into the Presence of God with an expectation to meet with God. So once he gets into his closet, he begins to interact with God.

Jesus taught us how to enter into God's Presence by following this model which is aimed at detailing the various components of an effective prayer:

> *"In this manner, therefore, pray:*
> *Our Father in heaven,*
> *Hallowed be Your name.*
> *Your kingdom come.*
> *Your will be done*
> *On earth as it is in heaven."*
>
> MATTHEW 6:9-10

Here, we see that God desires that His Kingdom comes to earth, but men ought to pray it into manifestation. Once God said, *'Thus says the Lord God: 'I will also let the house of Israel inquire of Me to do this for them...* (Ezekiel 36:37).

Consequently, God desires that the priest asks of Him on behalf of the people. As a priest, you need to learn how to present the needs of your family before the Lord. If you can learn to trust God with your family, He will grant you the desires of your heart. Prayer is a platform that allows two beings from two different realms: the Spiritual and the physical, to interact and commune together.

Therefore, let me emphasise here that the most fundamental essence of going into God's Presence is to have communion with Him. When you go to pray, brother, do not go selfishly because of your many family needs; the first purpose of prayer is to establish communion with God.

Communion is built on communication. Prayer is the first form of communication which breeds intimacy between you and God. As such, intimacy is the primary goal of prayer. Every husband needs to be close to God so that he can rightly tell God's counsel about his family. You need to know what God is saying about your children, your wife's business, and even your properties. Abraham was so close to God that God considered it a betrayal of trust to conceal a matter from His friend.

"And the Lord said, 'Shall I hide
from Abraham what I am doing.'"

GENESIS 18:17

Abraham raised altars of sacrifice to commune with God. Everywhere he went, he built altars to God which were expressions of communion with God. Every man should learn to build communion and intimacy, so that God may reveal His secrets to you. Once you have developed intimacy and built a consistent place and time of fellowship, you will not be caught unaware of critical matters that involve your family.

Deep secrets revealed are in the place of communion with God. God's secrets are what eyes have not seen, ears not heard, nor ever conceived in the hearts of men (I Corinthians 2:9). The Ability to know secrets gives you a vantage position when you need to make critical decisions that involve your family.

Dependence

Whenever a priest goes into the Presence of God, he does not perform his priestly duties like an expert in the business. Rather, in transacting with God Almighty, humility and total dependence on God is a critical posture of the heart that makes the priest get God's attention.

> *"Though the Lord is on high,*
> *Yet He regards the lowly;*
> *But the proud He knows from afar."*
>
> PSALMS 138:6

Our needs are insatiable. There is always still something to ask for—our needs are endless. We always depend on a superior authority to meet our needs. People can trust and rely on someone who can meet their needs. God is there for us in times of need. As children of God, He is the only person we can run to.

So, when you step out to pray with humility in your heart, what you are saying to God is, 'I am insufficient in myself; I need help.' Do not go into the Presence of God boasting and recounting all the things you have attained for yourself like the Pharisee in Jesus' parable (the parable merits mentioning).

Even though your wife might honour you as the leader and pastor of the home, you need to sincerely demonstrate to God through your thoughts, actions, words and deed that you depend on Him to run your family. When you are in the Presence of God in communion with Him, you must lean on Him. The reason you pray is that you are not self-sufficient. Hence, prayer from a humble heart is an avenue to declare your dependence on God.

The Kingdom of God

> '...your kingdom come...'
>
> MATTHEW 6:10

Now, the purpose of prayer is fulfilled when the needs of both parties are met. As a priest, understand that it is the will of God that His kingdom is established in your family. Therefore, one of your most paramount prayers should be that your life and your family will be yielded to the leading of the Holy Spirit and that you will be conformed to the image of Christ, so that you will be able to mirror heaven on earth.

Pray into the Future

"I do not pray for these alone, but also for those who will believe in Me through their word; that they all may be one, as You, Father, are in Me, and I in You; that they also may be one in Us, that the world may believe that You sent Me."

JOHN 17:20-21

As a husband, you do not wait until you see your children and grandchildren before praying them into purpose and fulfilment. If you are a person of God's Presence, you will understand that whatever God does with you is not just about you; God has a generation in mind.

While Jesus was on earth, He prayed for the church earnestly. He also prayed for people to become children of God and join the church. Jesus focused not only on the present but kept his eyes toward the future. He knew that in many years to come, people will arise and receive the gospel of the kingdom of God.

When God called Abraham, God was not thinking of just Abraham alone. He had a nation in mind, a new race of people to bear His name and be His people forever. God sees time from a generational and eternal perspective.

Therefore, as a praying priest, pray about the present and the future. Every man who stands as a priest in the home should learn to look beyond the present and rain seeds of prayers for the unborn.

THE TEACHING PRIEST

For a long time Israel has been without the true God, without a teaching priest, and without law.

2 CHRONICLES 15:3

Understand that priesthood is not only about praying and offering sacrifices. The priest also teaches the laws of God. Let us carefully pay attention to the order of the duties of the priest according to the scripture above.

Israel has been without:

- The true God
- A teaching Priest
- Law

In ancient Israel, the priest was a mediator between God and His people, and stood before God. To clarify, the priest saw the **true God** through His law (**Psalm 119:14-16**). As a result, the priest was the agent responsible for teaching God's law – the teaching priest.

The nation of Israel was in a state of anarchy and purposelessness when the prophet of God took the message of **2 Chronicles 15:3** to them. The people of Israel were serving strange gods that could not save them. In those times, Israel was without the knowledge of the true God. Hence, they were in a pathetic state of restlessness and turmoil.

Likewise, families without the knowledge of the true God will plunge into restlessness and turmoil, suffer from multiple afflictions and experience unexpected attacks from the gods of this age. Your responsibility as a priest is to teach both your wife and children who the true God is. Teach them God's law and His instructions. Teach them righteousness and holiness.

We do not need knowledge of a *god* in this age; we need knowledge of the true God. Like I mentioned previously, an understanding of the true God comes only by communion and abiding in His Presence. Therefore, all men who are husbands and husbands-to-be must not take God's Presence lightly. You have to learn to abide in the Presence of God and then lead others into His Presence. That is your surest security in this godless age.

Search the Scriptures

Now so it was that after three days they found Him in the temple, sitting in the midst of the teachers, both listening to them and asking them questions.

LUKE 2:46

During Jesus's ministry on earth, He had a vast knowledge of the scriptures. How was that even possible? An easy way to understand Jesus' depth of insight about the Word of God is to examine His passion to know all that was written in the scriptures. He became very conversant with the Word of God to the point that He knew when specific prophecies were fulfilled.

To know God and His ways, you have to know His Word. Job said that God's Word was more important to him than his necessary meals (**Job 23:12**). If only you can have this kind of disposition towards the Word of God, you will be quick to grow in the knowledge of God.

Learning the scripture may be difficult. Perhaps your schedule might seem tight. However, remember that learning the scriptures is not just for yourself but rather an expression of your ministerial duties to your wife and your family. Although no one will give you remuneration for studying the scripture, there are earthly benefits and eternal rewards for fulfilling your obligations to God.

Also, do not forget that priesthood is a selfless devotion, not a matter of convenience. The priesthood of Jesus was a sacrificial one. So also will yours be as a husband. You will sacrifice time, resources, and energy to make sure that your family gets an in-depth understanding of God's will and ways for their life.

Schedule time every day to stay in the Word of God. If you have difficulty understanding the scriptures, ask God to open your eyes of understanding (**Ephesians 1:17-18**). Persist in it and you will see a great transformation in your life.

Be an Example

"The former account I made,
O Theophilus, of all that Jesus began
both to do and teach."

ACTS 1:1

The best approach to teach is by living an exemplary life. During His days on earth, Jesus demonstrated the things He professed first so that He could present Himself as the model worthy of emulation. In this way, Jesus was able to speak into the life of His disciples.

For instance, if He wanted to teach about faith, He demonstrated faith first and then showed faith to His hearers. So teaching becomes an easy thing to do when your life speaks what you teach. Your wife will grow in faith if you demonstrate faith because iron sharpens iron. If your wife finds it difficult to pray, you need to show her how to pray. Tell her how you overcame the challenges of weariness and tiredness in prayer. Tell her about the great experiences you have had while spending time with God in prayer. When you humble yourself and show your wife the way to the Lord you instil belief within her.

Teach your family the ways of God through conspicuous examples. Teach them to do righteousness by being righteous yourself. Teach them to love by living a life built on love. Love your wife selflessly. Love your children and show them how to love too.

THE MEDIATOR

> "For there is one God and one Mediator
> between God and men, the Man Christ Jesus."
>
> I TIMOTHY 2:5

Here is the final duty of the husband as priest that I will share with you. So far, you have understood that priests go into the Presence of God bearing the desires of others in their hands to present to God. Those needs are not his alone. In the days of Zechariah, the husband of Elizabeth, he went into the Presence of God one day to offer incense to God. Zechariah did not go into the temple solely because of his personal needs. Instead, there was a whole congregation of people outside the temple who carried their needs. Zechariah went into the temple to address the needs of his people. (Luke 1:8-10)

Amazingly, when the angel of God visited Zechariah in the Presence of God that day, the angel announced to him:

> *"Do not be afraid, Zecharias, for your prayer is heard; and your wife Elizabeth will bear you a son, and you shall call his name John."*
>
> LUKE 1:13

God answered Zechariah's prayers when he least expected. One of the benefits of priesthood is that, when you put other people's needs above your own, God will take care of your needs as well. Do not ever forget that priesthood is a selfless devotion.

Whenever you stand in prayers for other people—your wife, children, relatives—you are partnering with Jesus in His eternal priesthood ministry to bring the will of God on the earth. So here is another vantage position where you can make intercession for your wife and children because of your inclination to the Presence of God.

> *"And the Lord said, 'Simon, Simon!*
> *Indeed, Satan has asked for you, that he*
> *may sift you as wheat. But I have prayed*
> *for you that your faith should not fail,*
> *and when you have returned to Me,*
> *strengthen your brethren."*
>
> LUKE 22:31-32

Can you see this dramatic event that took place in the spirit realm? Satan wanted to displace Peter but first, he needed permission. Satan wanted to harm him but thankfully, Jesus was also present. Jesus stood as the advocate for Peter that day and presented strong reasons why Peter should not be sifted. Jesus triumphed over Satan.

My sincere prayer for every man reading this book is that when the enemy seeks to attack your wife or any member of your family, may you not be idle. May you be in your priesthood office like Jesus and defeat the temptations against your loved ones.

Dear brother, God called you to be the priest in your home and conduct a critical ministry. May you receive the grace to carry out your priestly duties in your home!

5

LOVE
YOUR **WIFE**

CHAPTER FIVE

Love Your Wife

O ver the years, there has been great emphasis on financial and emotional stability when considering settling down in marriage. This emphasis is always backed with several examples cautioning that a man who cannot provide for his home is an infidel and not fit for marriage. Yet, even with financial stability, several marriages seem to be still shaking.

What could be the cause? Is there a greater need to be met? Have you ever wondered if there are any more tasks to be accomplished after providing for your family's basic needs and necessities? Yes, there is one more thing to do.

LOVE YOUR WIFE

"So husbands ought to love their own wives as their own bodies; he who loves his wife loves himself. For no one ever hated his own flesh, but nourishes and cherishes it, just as the Lord does the church."

EPHESIANS 5:28- 29

Loving your wife is a commandment you must observe with all diligence and sincerity. It is the solution to most problems and complications in marriage. A woman needs love most of all, and she responds to love without holding back. Therefore, love is a tool to wield success and joy in your marriage.

Your wife has plenty of wants, but she ultimately needs you. She does not want her husband to be represented by things: expensive presents and sophisticated technology. She needs reassurance and proof that you are still in love with her.

According to Dr. Myles Munroe, a woman, by design, is a receiver who will multiply everything you give her. When you give love to your wife, she receives it and multiples the love within your home.

TO WHAT EXTENT?

Many husbands will say, "I love my wife, and I care about her. However, she has hurt me, and now I am withdrawn. I will continue my show of love when she realises what she has done and rectifies it."

The scripture has already spelt out to what extent and in what manner you should love her.

The measure is not by how many times you are offended or how battered you are. Instead, it is in the way you attend and deal gently with yourself. Your wife is one with you. She has become your body.

Also, the Bible says:

> *"Husbands, love your wives,*
> *just as Christ also loved the church*
> *and gave Himself for her"*

EPHESIANS 5:25

Amazing right? You are to love your wife the same way Christ loves the church. How does Christ love us? He died for us while we were sinners. He didn't wait until we became righteous. He did not add a clause. Even after your mistakes, He came running after you and forgave you heartily without reminding you of your sins.

This is the extent to which you should love your wife.

HOW DO I EXPRESS LOVE TO HER?

Your expression of love to your wife goes beyond the public display of affection. It spans and transcends beyond the words of affirmation or costly gifts. You show love by investing in her. One of the greatest displays of love for your wife is in your daily sacrifice for her. She is your God-given garden, and you are the gardener.

WHAT IS A GARDEN?

According to Merriam Webster dictionary, a garden is a plot of ground where herbs, fruits, flowers, or vegetables are cultivated. It is also referred to as a rich well-cultivated region. This is who your wife is. She is your garden.

Who is a gardener? This is a person whose hobby and job is to grow a garden. If you grow vegetables professionally, you're called a farmer. But, if you design, tend, or care for a flower garden for pleasure, you're a gardener.

Fascinating! A gardener tends and cares for the garden for a lifetime. It is a lifetime occupation with numerous blessings attached to it. As a gardener, these are the things you should do to your garden:

Tend the Garden

To tend means to take care of or be in charge of someone or something. It also implies cultivating and serving as a caretaker of something or someone.

Your wife is not just your partner and lover; She is also your responsibility. A man of purpose will do everything possible to tend the garden the Lord committed into his care.

> *Then the Lord God took the man and put him in the Garden of Eden to tend and keep it.*

> GENESIS 2:15

How Do I Tend the Garden?

There are several ways to tend your garden. They include:

Giving her attention

Do you know why companies make large billboards and advertise on TV and radio? Companies advertise to get your attention. When they get your attention, you are more likely to buy the product, and this leads to high profit margins and overall growth.

YOUR WIFE IS YOUR GOD-GIVEN GARDEN, AND YOU ARE THE GARDENER

Everything and everyone wants your attention; however, your wife craves, desires, and deserves your attention more. She wants you to take notice of everything that is happening to her. For a garden to blossom, the gardener needs to pay close attention to what he has planted because that is the only way to identify what it needs.

When was the last time you took notice of your spouse? Did you notice when she changed her hairstyle? And are you aware when she is in pain? You can never know this if you are not attentive. Your wife deserves your attention every day. This sacrifice will, in turn, strengthen the bond of your relationship, and both of you will grow in happiness.

> But while men slept, his enemy came
> and sowed tares among the wheat and
> went his way.
>
> MATTHEW 13:25

Ignoring your wife wreaks havoc upon your life and communicates negativity and hatred towards her. She begins to feel that you no longer love her, and you don't find her attractive. Failing to cultivate your garden will affect her disposition and her response towards you. Resentment and bitterness will then begin to creep into the marriage like weeds into a flower bed.

Also, this may make your wife vulnerable to attacks. When she does not get attention from you, she may begin to find solace and comfort in someone else. Infidelity endangers your marriage because it may divert her attention and affection from you. Also, infidelity affects your sexual intimacy and gives space for the devil to steal the joy and peace of your home.

Listening to her

Unveiling your heart to your spouse and having access to hers requires listening attentively and well. With so many different problems, obligations, appliances and people pulling at us and clamouring for our attention, it can be challenging to slow down and truly listen to one another. Listening is beautiful, but sometimes it's tough.

Sometimes, you might want to tune out and bury yourself in your favourite pastime or dive into the bucket list of goals you wish to accomplish. In order to have a healthy, flourishing marriage, it's critical to listen to your spouse with true empathy and generosity.

One way to detect your wife is not happy with you is when she is quiet and not saying anything. Every woman loves to converse with her partner. She wants to talk about everything that happened to her that day. She does not know how to summarise words when she is with you, and you must listen. She wants you to journey with her by listening to her.

How Do I Listen To Her?

Listening to her is a deliberate act you must cultivate. You are not genuinely listening if it is void of these things:

1. Empathy and Emotion

Listen with empathy. It implies putting yourself in your wife's shoes and seeing things through her eyes without judging her from your own standpoint. Avoid offering solutions immediately, except she asks for your advice. Instead, listen with rapt attention. Listening will give you access to her deepest thoughts and her standpoint. Listening with empathy helps her feel secure, wanted, and loved.

It is easy to get blinded and be flooded by the torrent of your own emotions on the matter. The outcome of this action is you will inappropriately respond to your spouse. In order to avoid this, shut out your own emotions and listen to discern what your spouse is feeling.

Once you have identified what your spouse is feeling, whether it is pity, depression, anger, or excitement, it becomes easy to respond appropriately. You can adjust your responses based on her emotional state. This helps to keep communication healthy.

2. Rapt Attention

When communicating with your spouse, do not make it look like you are in a hurry to get to the end of the conversation. Use loving gestures and body language to let her know you are interested in what she is saying. Maintain eye contact and nod frequently to affirm what she is telling you. By paying rapt attention, you communicate your love for her. Additionally, you should also try to touch her passionately or hold her hands, turn your body toward her, drop your phone, newspaper and other gadgets, and stop what you're doing. This enables you to pay attention to her throughout the conversation.

At intervals, let her know that you are following and enjoying the conversation. Don't interject her, except she permits you to do so. Discern the emotion in her voice and give a suitable response when necessary. You don't need to have the same stance and uphold the same opinion. All you need is a little bit of compromise, wisdom, and patience.

3. Care for Her

No matter how strong your wife might look to outsiders and how effectively she attends to her various duties, she still needs your care. Yes, she is the mother of the home and knows how to care for everyone. Even though it seems like she is fine or she assumes a posture of confidence, she needs your compassion.

A gardener will not stop watering his plants because they are blooming and flourishing already. Instead, he will pay more attention to knowing the maturity date and when it needs to be pruned.

My pastor once told me a story of a woman who was angry with her husband because he didn't give her money. She had prayed to God to touch her husband's heart to give her money.

Then, one fateful day, her husband gave her a considerable sum of money based on the instruction of his pastor, and the woman burst into dancing, praising God. The husband was bewildered by the act, and then she narrated how she had been praying. The husband was surprised that his wife had been waiting for a day like that. His wife was earning triple his salary, which she only spent on herself because the husband provided for the family.

However, she felt it was cruel of her husband not to give her money for her upkeep though she earned more. All she wanted was a show of care and love from her husband.

If you care about your wife, you will labour diligently to provide for her and make her comfortable. A loving and caring husband is a hard-working husband. This doesn't mean that he has all the money, but his priority is to provide for his own.

Also, alleviate your wife of her burden so that she can have time for herself even if she never complains about doing the chores, your laundry, and preparing every meal for you and the kids. Make it a point of duty to serve her and ensure that she is taken care of just as she takes care of you. Give her a break. This will help to find refreshment, energy, and strength to carry on. The husband can learn to love and serve his wife in the home.

4. Fill Her Emotion Tank

Some psychologist have opined that women are emotional, and they respond to emotions swiftly. Always feed her emotions with the proper nutrition. Avoid saying words that will dampen her spirit. Instead, praise her. Do not criticise her or wait until she asks for it. Be ahead of her. Speak her love language to her constantly.

If her love language is receiving gifts, don't wait until special occasions like birthday or wedding anniversary to spoil her with presents. A gift is not just a price tag but also a representation of love. Always create a magical moment with her and prove to her that every moment counts. After tending to your garden regularly, you will see how these actions will change your relationship positively.

Guard the Garden

The gardener should carefully look for possible dangers and threats that will harm his garden. This is why he builds a fence around the garden to make it enclosed. The three most crucial duties of a husband are to oversee, procure and protect.

A man safeguards his spouse by providing a safe environment for her. He eliminates and reduces probable physical, emotional, or spiritual threats. Prevention is the most effective way to protect her from danger.

Every woman looks out for someone who will protect them. She loves to be cherished and wants to know that she is safe with you and you have her back. You become her father when you are married to her. She looks up to you for safety.

You might be thinking, what can I do after securing the environment and assigning guards? With proper security, she would be cared for when I am not around, right? No, there are many other things you still need to do. Those mentioned above are just a tiny fragment of your duties.

Protect her Emotions

Several factors pose serious threats to her emotional wellbeing. You must know what issues she is battling with, what is causing her pain, and find the means to stop them. Is she feeling inferior? Is she battling depression? Is she having a tough time at her workplace? Is she having difficulty in executing a project? You must find out by listening to her.

Once you identify the void in her heart, you can fix it more easily. You must always shield her from negativity and insecurities including the negativity and sin that exists with you. Know that since you are the most influential person in her life, you are the one who can do the most damage to her.

Nonetheless, consciously sowing good acts will reduce a lot of emotional damage. She is your lover and needs to be respected. Don't take advantage of her tenderness or trample upon her. She is created from your ribs, not from your feet. Seek her permission before having sex with her. She is not a toy.

Also, you can't emotionally abuse her and expect her to feel good about it. She must be aware of your fidelity and loyalty to her. Protect her from toxic relationships. Her productivity and joy may be tied to her relationships. What kind of friends does she associate with? Are they fuelling her strength or pulling her down? Are they helping her become who God wants her to be, or are they pulling her farther from God?

When you do this, you are also protecting your marriage. Protection will save your marriage from external intruders that are set to destroy your home. Moreover, some women worry a lot because they are anxious about the future. Minister to her fears and worries by encouraging emotional stability.

Be Her Covering

"For the husband is head of the wife, as also Christ is head of the church; and He is the Saviour of the body. Husbands, love your wives, just as Christ also loved the church and gave Himself for her, that He might present her to Himself a glorious church, not having spot or wrinkle or any such thing, but that she should be holy and without blemish."

EPHESIANS 5:23, 25- 27

Every man is the head of his own home. Just like Christ is the head of the church, you are both an administrative and spiritual head of your household. You are the watchman and the priest of your home. If something ails you, then your home becomes vulnerable. Remember, when the shepherd is struck, the flock will scatter.

You must seek the spiritual wellbeing of your wife. You are her spokesman and intercessor before God. God holds you accountable for the condition of your wife. Look at the account of Isaac and his son Jacob.

> *'Isaac was forty years old when he took Rebekah as a wife, the daughter of Bethuel the Syrian of Padan Aram, the sister of Laban the Syrian. Now Isaac pleaded with the Lord for his wife because she was barren, and the Lord granted his plea, and Rebekah his wife conceived.'*
>
> GENESIS 25:20-21

> *Now when Rachel saw that she bore Jacob no children, Rachel envied her sister and said to Jacob, 'Give me children, or else I die!' And Jacob's anger was aroused against Rachel, and he said, 'Am I in place of God, who has withheld from you the fruit of the womb?'*
>
> GENESIS 30:1-2

The Scriptures above show the state of the heart of Isaac and Jacob. It also reveals their understanding of their call and purpose as a husband. Isaac understood his duties and went on his knees to implore God for his wife. The Lord heard his cries and answered him swiftly.

It could be said that this experience changed Rebecca completely because when the children struggled within her, she did not scream or panic. Instead, she went to inquire of the Lord because her husband had shown her the way. She also knew that the way shown her worked. Rebecca asked of the Lord and got the plan of God concerning the twin in her womb (Genesis 25:22-23). How profound!

On the other hand, Jacob did not know the manner of man he was. He did not understand his duty as the man of the house. So, when his wife showed him the right way, he refused to listen. Instead, he was angry and spoke to her harshly (Genesis 30:1-2). How devastating!

This negligence of his duty led to the committing of a crime. His wife suggested that he should be intimate with his maid, Bilhah, and he obliged because he did not understand his ministry as a husband (Genesis 30:3). Nevertheless, the effect of his inadequacy didn't end there. See what the Bible says;

> *Now, Rachel took the household idols, put them in the camel's saddle, and sat on them. And Laban searched all about the tent but did not find them. And she said to her father, 'Let it not displease my Lord that I cannot rise*

before you, for the manner of women
is with me.' And he searched but did
not find the household idols.

GENESIS 31:34 -35

When Rachel could not find solace in Jacob's God, she stuck to her father's God. Although she stole the idols before the time this event took place, I believe that, if the response of Jacob had been the same as Isaac, Rachel would have responded just as Rebekah did.

She also lied to cover up her atrocity. When you don't stand your ground and express Christ to your wife and home, they will follow after strange gods and the lusts of their hearts.

How to be a Covering as a Husband

1. Lead Your Wife in Worship

A Christian husband seeks to walk in the steps of Christ. He constantly washes his wife with the washing of water, which is the Word. He continues in this life-long assignment of cherishing and nourishing her in the hope that she will be presented blameless to God when Christ appears the second time.

He leads her to develop a personal relationship with God and teaches her the doctrine of Christ, so that she may access grace, ask for help and receive mercy in a time of need. A real man is a man who provokes his wife to worship the true God. He encourages her to fellowship with God more by preaching God's Word. He does not drain her spiritual power; instead, he leads by example and reflects Christ to her. He are the pastor of the home.

2. Carry Your Wife's Burdens

Every husband is instructed by Apostle Peter to love their wife and to dwell with them in understanding (1 Peter 3:7). A loving husband will seek to be gentle toward his wife. Understand the times and seasons she finds herself in. Also, you must be willing to help her obey the instructions of the Lord. Don't insist on sexual intimacy when the Lord wants her to be separate for a while. Bear each other's burden and so fulfil the law of Christ.

The husband must not try to outshine his wife or stop her. Instead, look for ways to help her and see where to fit in, listen to her when the Lord commits a vision to her care, give her all the support she can get, and, most importantly, pray for her.

Deborah was a judge, and the wife of Lapridoth. She judged Israel for 40 years and led them to war alongside Barack. Lapridoth freely allowed his wife to do what the Lord had committed to her care.

Joseph understood God's intent for his wife, Mary and the role she had to play in delivering our Saviour, and he complied. The Bible says:

> *And did not know her till she had brought*
> *forth her firstborn son. And he called*
> *His name Jesus.*

MATTHEW 1:25

The above verse of the Bible shows a huge sacrifice Joseph made for his fiancée, Mary, who later became his wife and the mother of Jesus. Mary received the mandate to birth the Messiah while they were courting. Mary was a virgin, and they kept the marriage bed undefiled. However, when he became legally married to her, he refrained from touching her and being sexually intimate with her so that they could both successfully obey the Lord to the end.

He did not interfere the will of God with his burning desires. Also, Joseph took full responsibility for Jesus and followed the instructions of the Lord concerning Jesus' name, just as Mary was commanded. Joseph exemplifies a man who knows that the fulfilment of his wife's purpose is paramount. He went all out to ensure things worked out well according to God's plan.

3. Join Your Wife in Raising the Kids

A man is the spiritual head of the home, and he must teach his children about God and lead them to Christ. Set the example with family prayers and studying of the scriptures. Teach them how to live by faith. Don't trivialise the time for prayers and fellowship with God. If you do, your children will not take God seriously. You are their model so make sure to live in accordance with what you teach them. This will reduce the stress associated with raising children in a godly way.

Lead your family spiritually by reserving time to impart your children with Christian virtues. Also, teach them who a responsible man is. Treat your wife with care, and you would have succeeded in sharpening their perspective.

4. Be Her Defence

This implies that you should protect her name and stand up for her. There is nothing more despicable than allowing your wife to be trodden upon by your friends and family. Don't speak evil of her whether in her presence or behind her back. Each of her weaknesses and past are for your consumption alone. Do not discuss them with an outsider because she may find out. When she does, it will break her heart to know that you broke her trust and crack your marriage open.

Learn to appreciate each of her efforts and magnify her strengths. One thing you may not know about the Proverbs 31 woman is that it also speaks about her husband. He is a godly husband who does not gossip about his wife. He works diligently for his wife and children. He also praises his wife for all of her qualities before the other leaders in the city. The proverb concludes with these words: 'Let her works praise her in the gates' (Prov. 31:31).

> **RESERVE TIME TO IMPART YOUR CHILDREN WITH CHRISTIAN VIRTUES**

A loving husband will sing the praises of his wife in public (unless she is adamant that she doesn't like it when he does so). When you praise your wife, you are encouraging her and the attribute you highlight gets better. If you emphasise more on her mistakes, her mistakes gain prominence and become worse.

GROW AND PRUNE THE GARDEN

Growth is the process or a manner of increment and development in something or someone which is a vital part of everyone's life. In essence, growth is proof of vitality. When we are not growing, it is an indication that we are not healthy.

Marriage is more than just companionship, sexual intimacy, and reproduction. It is an avenue to grow. No one wants to cultivate a garden that will not grow, expand, and yield fruits. However, the garden will not grow as expected if you don't put in the necessary effort.

Every virtue you are seeing in your wife today was in seed form. Every prophecy the Lord has spoken about your wife is in seed form. However, if you are ready to water, expose the plant to sunlight and the right temperature, her virtues will grow.

Water

Every plant needs water to grow. Likewise, your wife needs the right word to grow. Your confession and your admonishment will spur her growth.

> *So now, brethren, I commend you to God and to the word of His grace, which is able to build you up and give you an inheritance among all those who are sanctified.*
>
> A C T S   20:32

What words are you sowing into the life of your wife daily? Do your words spur her to become the woman God has ordained her to be? Or do they pull her down and make her think less of herself?

Words, though intangible, are full of strength and power. Apostle James tells us that the power of life and death is in the tongue. So, you can either kill or heal her with your words. God gave us a vivid example of how to call things into existence. He showed us the power bestowed upon us as believers.

For every work God created, there is an underlying 'let there be'. You are a child of God. You have the same authority. How do you wield the tool the Lord has freely given you for your good? Hold back when you are not in the right frame of mind because words spoken in anger cannot be undone.

Does this mean I should not correct her? No, failure to correct her when she is wrong is sparing the rod and indicates that you don't love her as you profess. The child whom the father loves, he chastises. Correct her in love. Speak the truth in love. Be firm in your correction and, yet, mindful of her emotions.

She is first a child of God before she is your wife. She has the Holy Spirit. She loves God and you do not want to hurt Him. She loves you too and respects you. Correct her and show her what the Lord says about certain habits or mindset. Don't force or impose it on her. She is not your slave. She might disagree on an instance, but with time she will adjust. After you have pointed out her error to her, don't make a fuss out of it. Instead, let the Holy Spirit enlighten her.

Give her time to reflect on it and make changes. Let patience have its perfect work in your own life. Do you believe that your word will cause her to grow? Then don't panic when there are no changes yet. He that believes will not make haste.

Your plant will not show any sign of growth the exact day you watered it just as your seed will not grow the moment you bury it in the ground. However, one thing is certain; the seed will grow. It is the Lord that gives the increase, not man. This is the wisdom of God, not of man. Let God do His work.

Sunlight

Every plant needs sunlight. Sunlight helps the plant grow well and produce its food itself through a process called photosynthesis. When a plant no longer has access to sunlight, it begins to wither and die. What are you exposing your wife to? Are they things that aid her growth or do they defile her conscience?

You are the gateway to your wife. If your way is not right with God, it will affect her output and prosperity. It is beyond your words. It is about your overall lifestyle.

Introduce a new perspective to her, and she will accept it without questioning because she trusts you with her life and reveres you as the supreme head in the house. However, if your doctrine is faulty, you will influence her negatively. When Abraham told Sarah to pretend she was his sister instead of identifying herself as his wife, she did not fight it because she was subject to him. Unfortunately, this decision would have exposed her to adultery if God had not intervened.

Always promote goodness within her and discourage evil, which will cause her to whither like untended flowers in the garden. Exposing your wife to evil may cause her to lose connection with God and fall prey to the devil. Always refer her to God.

Temperature

Every garden needs the right temperature to function well as it ought to. If the temperature is not conducive, it will affect the fruitfulness of the plant. Likewise, your wife needs the right atmosphere to thrive and grow.

This atmosphere could be spiritual, emotional, or physical. Is your wife eager to come home from work? Is home hell for her or another heaven on earth? Does her heart skip for joy when she sees you, or does it beat with fear? It is saddening that churches mostly talk about the nagging wife without talking about the abusive husband.

Your wife should smile when she thinks about you and not the other way around. When the atmosphere is right, she will receive every other nutrient generously without questioning. However, when it is not, she becomes sceptical about every good intention.

Prune the Garden

Pruning is the act of removing dead and dying branches, allowing room for new growth. It also deters pests. Pruning is not a wicked act but a sincere display of love. Don't shy away from it.

See what the Bible says;

> *"Every branch in Me that does not bear fruit*
> *He takes away; and every branch that bears*
> *fruit He prunes, that it may bear more fruit."*
>
> JOHN 15:2

Amazing right? Pruning is something God does Himself. He enforces this act on everyone who loves Him and keeps His commandment. Similarly, pruning your garden is an act of love that is orchestrated by God.

A proper prune is both an obligation and a long term investment in the plant itself. Proper pruning is tending to your spouse's future and doing everything within your might to ensure she gets there safely. So, you take a step further by planning a safe landing for her.

See this example from the Bible:

> *"And Mordecai told them to answer Esther: Do not think in your heart that you will escape in the King's palace any more than all the other Jews. For if you remain completely silent at this time, relief and deliverance will arise for the Jews from another place, but you and your father's house will perish. Yet who knows whether you have come to the kingdom for such a time as this."*

ESTHER 4:13-14

This story is one that you should know well from the Bible: the story of Mordecai, Esther's Uncle. Mordecai had been the father figure in her life from birth. When Esther became wife to the King, Mordecai knew it was beyond the luxury of the moment. He saw a future that Esther knew nothing about and reminded her when it was time to carry out the eternal counsel of God.

Esther could not see what was ahead and why the Lord had raised her. However, Mordecai knew because he had cared for her. When Mordecai found out about the decree spearheaded by Haman to kill all the Jews, he tore his clothes. He sat in the middle of the city and cried with a loud voice. He refused to be comforted, knowing what was at stake. Esther sent him luxurious things, thinking that was why she had become queen, but she was naive. Mordecai refused her gifts and focused on pruning her without bias or mincing words.

He told Esther that God had a plan for her. He shed off her excesses, changed her mindset, and restructured her. He showed her the danger of not being trimmed and made her know that there are several replacements if she refuses to bear fruit.

Though this act seemed very tough on both of them, the outcome changed the narrative for the Jews. Esther fulfilled the course for which she was raised which led to triumph over their enemy.

As a man, you have oversight over your wife. You are the intercessor between her and God. You must listen to what the Lord is saying about her. Then, make it a daily habit to help her shed off the weight. This will help her reach the goal faster.

Just as a painter will adjust his drawings with brushes until the drawings match the picture in his mind, you must prune your garden to bear much fruit. Although pruning is hard on both the garden and the gardener, the result is profitable for both.

_6_

THE **CALL**

CHAPTER SIX

The Call

S o much has been said about the man: who he is, and the role he plays. However, there is a side to the man that encapsulates all other aspects of him. Man does not only have roles to play in the home, but he also has a divine call from God to fulfil as a husband.

Have you ever wondered about your calling as a husband? Maybe you have been questioning yourself as to whether you are fulfilling divine assignment as head of the home? Do you think you have not lived up to God's expectation for you as a husband?

In this last chapter, these and many other questions will be answered.

THE CALLING OF THE HUSBAND

Lover

You will not normally encounter the joining of a man and a woman as husband and wife without the existence of love between them. Most times, the love at the beginning may not feel the same after some years into the marriage. But you need to understand that what keeps marriage is beyond initial infatuation. As a husband, you might find your wife's physical beauty begins to fade over the years, which can cause you to start to question your love for her.

When your wife starts to look unattractive to you, it is time to love her intentionally. Yes, love can be intentional. Remember those beautiful things you did for your wife when you first met her: those words of hope and affirmation you told her often and the romantic moments shared together. If your wife's happiness matters to you, then you need to revive those things again.

God has committed another life into your hands, and you need to take good care of it. Your wife is you in another body, but in marriage, you become one flesh. Just as you love your own body, love your wife in the same manner. Your wife owns the solemn right to enjoy romantic moments with you and not anyone else. Do not ignore your wife when she needs you the most. Also, always let her know how much you love her both in words and in deeds.

Love has been defined in many ways by different people of different races and ideologies. However, your knowledge of God's disposition to love will help you understand what love entails. First John chapter 4 verse 7 says,

> *'Beloved, let us love one another, for love is of God; and everyone who loves is born of God and knows God. He who does not love does not know God, for God is love.'*

1 JOHN 4:7-8

The Scripture tells us that God is love. In God, Love is personified. Most times, the term love is only taken as a feeling and nothing more. So, you hear some say 'I love you, and others feel 'Love is blind'. This is now a cliché. But God, through His Word, says that love is more.

> JUST AS YOU LOVE YOUR OWN BODY, LOVE YOUR WIFE IN THE SAME MANNER

Love is beyond having feelings for the other; it is a personality. God is love. The more you regard spiritual things, like love, as ordinary, the more you may miss out on being able to love genuinely. Not all are capable of loving the God-kind-of-way, which is the right way. You cannot claim to love God and hate your brother (1John

4:20). You cannot claim to love your wife and hate every beautiful thing and people around her that give her joy.

Now, there are specific characteristics of love, as explained through God's word.

> 'Love suffers long and is kind; love does not envy; love does not parade itself, is not puffed up; does not behave rudely, does not seek its own, is not provoked, thinks no evil; does not rejoice in iniquity, but rejoices in the truth; bears all things, believes all things, hopes all things, endures all things.'
>
> I CORINTHIANS 13:4-7

These characteristics of love in the text above show how God has chosen that love be expressed among brethren. It is impossible to love when you are not kind. Being kind-hearted alone is not enough. Any relationship based on body chemistry will soon fade because emotions are not stable. What you think or feel is love might not actually be it. You might like her dress style, her hair, and manner of speech and so on. But these are not enough to build a lifelong relationship. When those things fade away, what remains for you to love? There is more to love. At the end of the day, it is the heart that has the characteristics written in 1 Corinthians 13 that matters.

To love is to bear whatever that comes along with the object of love; to believe and hope and be ready to face any outcome confidently. To love is to put an end to selfishness and become a man who lives a sacrificial life. To love is to see iniquity and not be angry with the person because you also see and acknowledge our human frailties, uphold truth, and develop trust at all times. Love is a mystery which many are yet to unravel.

> 'Husbands, love your wives, just as
> Christ also loved the church and gave
> Himself for her.'

EPHESIANS 5:25

Among many other divine calls, God chooses you and calls you to be the lover in the home. This call is way beyond mere feelings. It is a call to bring the husband to the measure of Christ's love. What, then, is the standard of Christ's love? The answer is in John 15:13: 'Greater love has no one than this; to lay down one's life for his friends.' What a great act of sacrifice! God's love is far above human comprehension.

In the same manner that Christ loves the church, husbands are to love their wives. This is more than an instruction: it is a command. 'HUSBANDS, love your wives...' God did not say you should try to love. He didn't say you should endeavour to love. He plainly commanded through this statement: 'Husbands love your wives.' What a great God! How marvellous are His works!

Also, in love is kindness found. God demands that the husband be kind towards his wife and family. He should not be a miser who withholds acts of generosity for self-interest. Be generous to your home. Give to your family freely, not under compulsion but as an expression of love.

Subsequently, challenges become inevitable as you go on in the marriage. You will begin to see some things that could break the home. However, it is at those times that you, as the husband, need to step into your office. No running away! No backing out! The communion of marriage is a lifelong commitment. Even when a fallout in the home seems imminent, you must do your best to restore love and orderliness. God has committed so much into your hand as the man of the house. You must always stand up to your responsibilities.

To be a lover, you are to pattern your life after God's Word. Since God has called you to love, He expects you to love the right way. To truly love the right way, you must learn to love God. Through your love of God, you will be able to sincerely love your wife.

Builder

The family is a home. You build it by putting one brick over another. Everyone in the home has their duties, but the husband is the main builder. While your wife supports you as the pillar in the house, you are called to construct your family by taking into consideration God's plain for your home.

The moment you were joined together as husband and wife, God gave the master plan to you as the head of the home. You are to build your home following God's standard. How then can you know God's standard as the husband? You can know it only through God's Word.

The Bible says:

> 'Unless the LORD builds the house,
> they labour in vain who build it; unless
> the LORD guards the city, the watchman
> stays awake in vain.'

PSALMS 127:1

Building a home without God is futile and will never amount to anything meaningful. The husband must learn to partner with God in building the home. You can never partner with God and build incorrectly.

The moment we take the marriage vows and agree to live as husband and wife, God becomes a witness to the vow between us, so we need to build the home bearing God's intent for marriage in mind. God wants to be involved in how we run our homes right from the onset of the marriage. He is there when we start it and will see us through till the end, if only we will depend on Him. In Jeremiah chapter 29 verse 28, the Bible says, *'Build houses and dwell in them; plant gardens and eat their fruit.'*

Unfinished tasks displease God; neither does He delight in uncompleted buildings. Whatever God starts, He finishes (Roman's 9:28). Even though God desires to make homes a place of rest, peace, and paradise on earth, many homes are not built according to God's original design. Such homes that ignore the will, presence and leadings of the Master-builder, God, open their doors for troubles.

For instance, a home where the wife raises her voice at every slightest misunderstanding or the man abuses his wife, is not ordered after God's design. Such homes feel uncomfortable to dwell in, and the children will never enjoy the peace within them. What a pity! The chain of ill-planned and distorted homes repeat from generation to generation unless broken. A man's life becomes miserable when his home is not at peace.

Dear husband, build your home the right way if you want to look back and smile at your work at your old age. The joy, happiness, peace, and love in the home are on the builder— the husband. Build according to plan, and your family can be counted as a standard for other generations.

> ## A MAN'S LIFE BECOMES MISERABLE WHEN HIS HOME IS NOT AT PEACE

Subsequently, the place of the home is essential in nation-building. A home is an institution. If it is wrongly built, it produces uncultured, unlearned and ill-mannered citizens in the society, which stunts the growth of a nation. As a husband, you are called to be a builder. You have a responsibility, which is to build your home. Build a man, you have built a leader; but build a home, you have built a nation.

> *"Now if anyone builds on this foundation*
> *with gold, silver, precious stones, wood, hay,*
> *straw, each one's work will become clear;*
> *for the Day will declare it, because it will be*
> *revealed by fire; and the fire will test each*
> *one's work, of what sort it is."*
>
> I CORINTHIANS 3:12-13

As inspired by the Lord in the Scripture above, Apostle Paul spoke about building on a foundation. According to the Word of God, the sure foundation is Jesus Christ (2 Timothy 3:16). Let Christ be the foundation of your home, and you are sure to experience peace even when the storm of life blows. Every home must be built on a solid rock that never loses its strength. What use is a building whose foundation is weak? You do not need a prophet to tell you that homes built on weak and inappropriate foundations will soon collapse.

As we carefully study the book of first Corinthians chapter 3, it is expedient to know the materials needed to build a home rightly. It is your responsibility as a husband to provide the appropriate materials for building the home even after making Jesus the home's foundation.

When materials that are of good quality and are durable are used to build, the building becomes strong and it is able to withstand challenges that the climate might pose to it. In like manner, regardless of how perfect any home might look on the outside, there is never a home without challenges. What determines whether your home will stand or fall amid those challenges is the principles you use to build.

The proper material for building the home is in God's Word.

The Bible says:

"But the fruit of the Spirit is love, joy,
peace, longsuffering, kindness, goodness,
faithfulness, gentleness, self-control.
Against such, there is no law."

GALATIANS 5:22-23

One of the essential materials in building your home is love. When love is absent from home, crisis soon follows. A home without love is like a moving vehicle without the driver. Undoubtedly, the end of such a home can be disastrous. Love keeps all things in proper flow within the home.

The fruit of the Spirit is the authentic character of God in man. You cannot have the nature of God and not have a blissful home. God is love. In His love, he bears all things and does not react based on the behaviour of man. God does not take hurt by your actions. All of Him is all love. Likewise, a man needs to build his home on this kind of character.

"For every house is built by someone,
but He who built all things is God."

HEBREWS 3:4

The choice to build your home is yours as a husband. Also, the materials to use are available at your disposal.

Nevertheless, no man can build without the Spirit of God. No one fails after they put God first. Give God first place even as you build your home. Involve Him in your everyday dealings.

Your responsibility as a builder requires you put your trust and confidence in God to guide you all the way. You might be aware of the suitable materials needed, but God is more aware of how, where and when to use the materials. Take solace in the fact that God is willing to help you if you let Him. Your responsibility as a home builder is God-given. Accept, cherish and walk worthy of this calling.

Shepherd

"He will feed His flock like a shepherd;
He will gather the lambs with His arm,
and carry them in His bosom, and gently
lead those who are with young."

ISAIAH 40:11

Who is a shepherd? What does a shepherd do? How is your calling as a husband likened to that of a shepherd?

Among many other responsibilities of a husband, being a shepherd stands out. There is no shepherd without a flock. A shepherd is someone who does not only lead the sheep but cares for them, feeds them, protects them and nurtures them all through their growing age.

As a husband, your call is similar to the shepherd who tends his flock. You feed your family. A husband who cannot provide for his family is not worthy of being called a man. Laziness is not an excuse for a husband. Your physical strength as a man was given for this purpose. God told Adam that he would have to till the ground to feed his family (Genesis 3:23). There is no excuse for not being a good shepherd because all that makes you a shepherd as a man has been built into you.

Beyond providing sustenance, you should also provide food for the spirit. The spirit thrives on the Word of God and allows your family to grow in God. You are the bishop, the priest, and the teacher at home. You should feed your family with the knowledge of God's Word. But how can you feed another when you have nothing in your store?

Feed your spirit. Your knowledge of God's Word must be grounded for you to feed your family well. Study to show yourself approved unto God (2 Timothy 2:15). You can only feed your home out of the abundance you have. Therefore, invest time in studying the Word of God, and feed your home out of the fullness you have.

Also, a good shepherd is a good leader. Being the head of the family is a call to leadership and responsibility. Leadership comes at a cost. At times, you will have to be at the forefront of some fierce battles against your home and take the responsibility to fight victoriously.

God has called you to be like His son Jesus, the good shepherd. Therefore, your number one and only model as a husband is Jesus Christ. He is the head and saviour of the church, which is His body (Ephesians 5:23b). To understand your duty as a shepherd, you must study Jesus. He is the perfect example of a shepherd since he is the Shepherd and Bishop of our souls.

Jesus said:

> *"I am the good shepherd. The good shepherd gives His life for the sheep. But a hireling, he who is not the shepherd, one who does not own the sheep, sees the wolf coming and leaves the sheep and flees; and the wolf catches the sheep and scatters them."*
>
> JOHN 10:11-12

The good shepherd gives his life for the sheep. That means a lot! No one is saying you should offer your body as a burnt offering for your family. Not at all! Jesus has already paid the highest sacrifice. Instead, God loves that you accept your role as a husband. Accept your call wholeheartedly, and walk in it through a life of sacrifice, consecration, and commitment towards the growth and development of your home. You are to protect them, pray for them, and lead them as the shepherd of your home. You must lead till the end.

But then, how can you be a good shepherd if you cannot hear the voice of God—through His Word, His audible voice and through other brethren in the faith— since God is the husband's head and the husband is the head of the home? Following God allows a husband to be a good shepherd. Therefore, your actions must follow the will of God, your heavenly Father.

You will go into diverse errors if you continuously walk in self-made wisdom (Proverbs 13:20). Except you are led by God, you will not lead right. Your tutelage under God's leadership is a model for you to lead your home.

The home is in danger when the husband can't hear the voice of God for his family. Your choices, decisions and actions should always find its root in God. I am always surprised to hear Christians say they cannot hear from God. The next question I ask them is, when last did you study your Bible? Often, they say a few weeks ago, a month ago or sometimes on Sundays alone.

You can see why it becomes impossible for such people to hear God's voice. There is nothing God would say to you today that He hasn't said in His Word. Your responsibility as a husband who wants to hear God's voice is that you search the Scriptures.

Excellence comes from God's Word. Right judgements and decisions are in His Word. Unless you learn of Him rightly, you cannot lead rightly. You are first a Christian before you become a husband. Therefore, as much as your home is your responsibility, you are accountable to God. God's Word cannot be overemphasised in your position as a shepherd. You are to consume His words and understand His sayings. His words are yes and amen (Revelations 3:14). God's words are undisputed and undiluted. To be a good shepherd, you have to be a man of God's Word.

Consequently, a good shepherd does not run away from responsibility. The truth remains that that responsibility is yours to handle. To shy away from responsibility is to deny who you are. Never turn away from your calling because it will give you fulfilment in life and destiny.

However, being responsible does not guarantee that you will have a smooth ride in your marriage. Leadership is not without challenges. But as long as you update yourself daily with the Word of God and obey Him, be rest assured of victory. This is where many go into error. They resort to what is not in God's Word. God did not promise a challenge-free life. However, He promised that in Him you would overcome (John 16:33). Hence, as a Christian, you must face every form of challenge with the confidence that you will win.

The Scriptures say:

> *"Thus says the Lord God: 'Behold, I am against the shepherds, and I will require My flock at their hand; I will cause them to cease feeding the sheep, and the shepherds shall feed themselves no more; for I will deliver My flock from their mouths, that they may no longer be food for them."*
>
> EZEKIEL 34:10

An example of an irresponsible shepherd is seen in the above scriptures. Even though they knew they were called to be shepherds, they misused every opportunity and turned the sheep's heart against their Maker.

Dear husband, you will give an account of your call as a shepherd, just the same way God demanded from these people. Live and act in accordance with the Word of God that you may stand confident in the day of accountability. You are not to be afraid because God is good, and He is with you always. Glory to God! He has appointed you and given you the role of a shepherd over your home and family. You must lead them towards what is good by teaching them what is right, and by caring for them.

Leader

> *"But I want you to know that the head of every man is Christ, the head of the woman is man, and the head of Christ is God."*

> I CORINTHIANS 11:3

There is a familiar maxim which goes thus: 'To whom much is given, much is expected.' The husband has been given much to do and if he truly wants to live up to his call, he must come to a full awareness of all that has been committed to him. The knowledge of who he is and what he is called to do is of utmost importance. Understanding the reasons behind all these is as necessary as having a foreknowledge of who you are called to be. Being the head of a family is like having a blank cheque, you have to put a pen to it, in this case the garment of leadership, and write out what you want to see. It is a call to serve.

The leader of the home is the husband. It will be outright irresponsibility to pass the baton on to the wife; it is not her duty. That is how God designed it, and that is the way it should be. A tweak or change in duty is to go against God's will.

In the text above, direct comparisons were made to depict the leadership of the husband. As God is head over Christ, Christ is head over man. Therefore, God made man (husband) the head of his woman (wife).

Your responsibility as the head is to lead. Once the duty of leadership is taken away, headship ceases. This is true in any organisation, ministry, or group. It is the sole responsibility of the head, in every sphere, to lead. It is impossible to have two leaders in a group or organisation (Matthew 6:24). If any of such exists, then you do not need faith to know that such an organisation or group will soon fail. Too many cooks spoil the broth, just as two leaders cannot lead simultaneously in any organisation. Either one steps down for the other, or the organisation crashes.

The husband and wife cannot hold the position of the head at home simultaneously in order to avoid conflict of ideas or opinion. God did not create the home to be a place of confusion and division, which is why the Scriptures clearly state that the head is the man. The responsibility to lead is given to one person. Leadership is not for all. As the husband, you are the leader. You are to lead your home as Christ leads the church.

"But the father said to his servants, 'Bring out the best robe and put it on him and put a ring on his hand and sandals on his feet. And bring the fatted calf here and kill it, and let us eat and be merry; for this, my son was dead and is alive again; he was lost and is found.' And they began to be merry."

LUKE 15:22-24

Leadership is responsibility and accountability. It is wrong to pass blame onto others as a leader. To claim that every mistake made is not your fault and every setback encountered is due to your members' inefficiency is wrong. The father (a representation of God) in Luke 15 took upon himself the pain of waiting daily outside his house if by any means his prodigal son would return. However, the child willingly chose the path to destruction.

Despite the error of the child, the father understood that he was accountable for both boys and would not give up on them. He chose not to lose hope. He must have been praying for the son daily as he anticipated for his return. Fathers must therefore acknowledge that it may be impossible to keep our progenies from committing wrongdoings. Hence, the important and crucial thing is that we play our part well and rightly. This is one of the significant reasons the husband must be close to God.

Daily, build an intimate relationship with the Leader of all, God Almighty. It is only through our acquaintance with Jesus that we can genuinely learn of God.

The Scriptures say:

> *"Come to Me, all you who labour and are heavy laden, and I will give you rest. Take My yoke upon you and learn from Me, for I am gentle and lowly in heart, and you will find rest for your souls."*
>
> MATTHEW 11:28-29

You need God to lead your home in a way that pleases Him. He chose you to be the leader. He understands quite well the nitty-gritty of leadership in the home better than anyone else. You will only be a true leader in your family when you surrender totally to God's leadership.

In leadership, making comparisons is wrong. You do not have to compare or compete. Your standard is Christ, and it is Him you must look up to at all times. Every man has been given equal but unique responsibilities. God would not provide you with something which He cannot help you handle. If He has given you responsibility, then He's expecting you to trust Him in it. God expects that you rely on Him in managing the affairs of your life and home.

Consider this question that Jesus asked His followers while He was teaching:

"And He spoke a parable to them:
Can the blind lead the blind?
Will they, not both fall into the ditch?"

LUKE 6:39

Even though you are called to lead your home as a husband, you will lead your family into error if you are not aware of how to go about it. Ignorance is a form of darkness. Unless you live your life in the light of God's Word, an ignorant husband will end up leading his family into troubles. God's Word has been made available to every man. It is within your reach. So tap into the light available for you.

Warrior

"Blessed be the Lord my Rock, who trains my
hands for war, and my fingers for battle."

PSALMS 144:1

King David had spent most of his childhood tending his father's flock. While his brothers joined the army of Israel, he was going about the duty of being a shepherd. It is incredible to realise that an outcast shepherd, forgotten even by his father, became a warrior and a king. How could he have been one, except he was trained by the

Lord? How could he have prospered unless he obeyed the Lord wholeheartedly?

One important role you must fill as the husband is that of a warrior. You are to stand in the gap for your family and ensure your city (home) is kept safe. Issues, challenges and uprisings are bound to happen in the home. Even Jesus, while on earth had His share. To assume challenging times are not likely to happen is to give a grand entry for them to come in. These challenges that stand as mountains will surely surface. It is your duty to fight and defeat them.

If the head of the home is the weakling in the family, it is a disappointment before God and man. In order to avoid such tragedies, you are to stand accountable for every member of your family. As the head, your members will be requested at your hand. When faced with these trials, your role as a warrior should sound an alarm to you. Each challenge is a call to fight. Husband, you must war!

As a Christian, your knowledge of being a warrior is not sufficient for your journey to victory on the battlefield. David, whenever faced with war, did something remarkable as part of his preparation to battle.

The Bible says:

> "So David INQUIRED of the Lord, saying,
> 'Shall I pursue this troop? Shall I overtake

them? "And He answered him, 'Pursue,
for you shall surely overtake them and
without fail to recover all."

I SAMUEL 30:8

At every point before any fight, David always inquired from God what to do. The question in his heart was always: 'What is the Lord's view about this one?' He understood this principle of asking God before taking action.

You need to have a clear grasp of when to fight and when to maintain peace. There will be times when the situation may look fierce, but the Lord will not call you to act. Also, there could be times when everything may seem calm, but the Spirit of God will tell you to pray. Your ability to distinguish between these two situations is essential for the joy of your home.

A warrior who wants to conquer must inquire of God. The husband who wants to triumph must seek God's counsel at all times. Seeking God's view about every matter brings delight to Him. This act proves to God that you solely depend on Him. God will in turn prove to you that no one relies on Him and comes to shame. He takes it as His responsibility to help you all the way because of your solemn act of acknowledgement.

Your tactics and weapons will determine the outcome of every battle. Loss or victory rests upon using the right weapon. For instance, wisdom is a necessary weapon for winning wars (Ecclesiastes 9:18). Every husband must be a man of wisdom. Without wisdom, you cannot win. Additionally, prioritising God is true wisdom.

God is first. You must note that it is through wisdom that you must wage your war (Proverbs 24:6). An unwise man will try to be self-dependent in his understanding. Wisdom teaches you to go to God. Wisdom directs you to seek God's face at every turn. There are different types of wisdom (James 3:17). A warrior must learn to lean on God's wisdom.

Awareness of your enemy in the fight requires wisdom. It is not enough to have information about your assignment; you also need to know your enemy.

The Scriptures say:

> *"For we do not wrestle against flesh and blood, but against principalities, against powers, against the rulers of the darkness of this age, against spiritual hosts of wickedness in the heavenly places."*
>
> EPHESIANS 6:12

Your fight is not against the lady next door or the older woman down the street. Every problem has its root in the spirit realm. Your fight is spiritual. To fight spiritual battles, you must wage spiritual war. The Word of God has plainly outlined those who are against the progress and development of your home. The devil is the enemy, and it is your duty as the husband to eradicate him from your home.

How can you wage spiritual warfare if you do not know how to pray? When your strength fails, you will be at a dead-end if you are a prayerless husband. A praying husband is a man of war. To effectively fight, you must pray. Your effectual and fervent prayer is bound to break yokes (James 5:16).

Of course, bodily exercise profits little (1Titus 4:8). Beyond building physical muscles as a man, you need to develop spiritual stamina. You might not be a man of huge muscles physically, but it will be detrimental to you and your family if you are weightless in spirit.

It is God's will that you are used as an instrument in taking territories. You are responsible to God and your family. You are to seek Him daily for direction and strategy and lean on Him to equip and uphold you even as you wage war against every enemy. Your spiritual strength determines the strength of your family. Every husband has been anointed as a prophet in the home. You must go home and bring deliverance to your family. You are to fight and not to be an onlooker. You are a warrior!

Provider

Once there was a couple who disagreed on who would provide for the home. The wife had her clear points from Genesis that God gave Adam work to provide for his family.

On the other hand, the husband would dodge her points by likening her to the woman in Proverbs 31. He would say that as an industrious wife, she did not have to wait for the husband before seeing to the needs of the home. This caused constant complaints in the home.

The question now is, 'Who should provide for the home?' To avoid heresies, we have to take a cursory look at the Scriptures.

> *'But if anyone does not provide for his own,*
> *and especially for those of his household,*
> *he has denied the faith and is worse than*
> *an unbeliever.'*

> I TIMOTHY 5:8

It is no coincidence that a man was referred to in the above Scripture. There is no mistake in God, and His works are perfect. The Scripture clearly states that a man (in this context, husband) who does not provide for his home (see to their everyday need) has turned against his faith in the Lord Jesus. Such a man is worse than one who never believed God. What an abounding misery to such a person!

God authorises the husband as the provider in the home. Having cleaved to your wife, you must make necessary provisions for your home whenever need arises. You cannot hold your wife responsible to provide even if she earns more money than you or spends a lot.

Of course, many wives would like to help their husbands, especially when they earn more. This is an excellent thing to do, but not for a lazy man who is unwilling to work and provide for his home. The truth of the matter is that God would have said it through His Word if the wife was meant to be the provider.

There could be a consensus between the husband and the wife for a specified period. It could be due to financial challenges in the home. At those times, the wife should help. This does not mean it has become her responsibility. She only agreed to that because she is the wife (a helpmeet).

Every husband has been called to be a provider and must live up to their call. You will be in error to lapse in this your God-given role. Once the acknowledgement of your role in the home is absent, you have shown yourself to be ignorant and destruction is inevitable (Hosea 4:6). There is no advantage in ignorance. Whether you are aware or not, you will receive the consequences of your actions if you go against the set law. God requires of you as a husband to be the provider.

You are to wake up each morning with this understanding that your family needs you to provide for them. This does not endorse laxity from the wife. It only approves that you do your responsibility as unto the Lord.

You will discover that being a provider will earn you the respect needed to keep being the head of the family. The one who provides is the head. A teacher is the head of the class because the teacher provides knowledge to the students.

In contrast, a man ceases to be the head of the family once he abdicates his responsibility to provide for the home. God has chosen you as the head of the family (Ephesians 5:23). You must live up to this call by responding duly to your responsibilities.

Notwithstanding, you have nothing to worry about. The One who has called you has made provisions for you. God wants you to look up to Him as your head the same way you want your wife and children to look up to you as the head of the home. Look up to God almighty to help you regarding your role in the family. God never fails (Luke 1:37). You can be sure that help is always available for you.

In conclusion, God made you a man, and He never made a mistake about that. How God designed you is perfect, and everything you need to live a fulfilled life as a man has been wired into you. However, being just a man is not enough to fulfil your assignment on earth. God wants you to rise to the position of head of your home—a husband.

The husbandman must live to fulfil his ministry to his family and the nation at large. When you step up, God will surely step in.

OTHER BOOK
BY THE AUTHOR

FOREWORD BY **BISHOP EMILY BUABASAH**

THE
MINISTRY
OF THE

Wife

Understanding Your Calling

DOUGLAS ASANTE

GRAB
YOUR
COPY

A V A I L A B L E   O N

amazon   amazon kindle   audible

www.equippublishing.co.uk